Water Gardens

SIMPLE STEPS FOR ADDING THE BEAUTY OF WATER TO YOUR GARDEN

TIME
LIFE
BOOKS

ALEXANDRIA, VIRGINIA

Water Gardens

Introduction

Water gardens furnish the outdoor environment with distinctive sights and sounds that are soothing yet stimulating at the same time. The gentle trickle of a fountain and the energy of a gurgling stream both utter a primordial call that most of us can't resist. They urge us to come closer, to sit and ponder, or simply to relax and observe the world in a microcosm.

Where there is a fountain or waterfall, there is also an endless fascination in the water's movement. In a still pond, we can watch fish swim and catch the reflection of garden plants. If we add a variety of plants into and around a water garden, we inject more complexity into its world. At once it is a larger habitat for wildlife, though dependent on the gardener for ecological stability. Where space and time allow, you can combine fish with submerged and surface plants that cooperate in a perfectly balanced environment. Rather than maintaining equilibrium in a naturalistic pond, however, many gardeners will prefer a filtration system and a crystal clear pool.

Whatever your taste, it's important to identify the physical limits and to plan details carefully so that your new water feature becomes an integrated part of the existing landscape and remains problem free. This book will guide you in choosing a style among various types of water gardens that is right for you. When you're ready to plunge into your project, work through the detailed step-by-step instructions to create your water garden, and then use the numerous plant guides to help select the best accents for a water feature that will give you a lifetime of enjoyment. ❧

Getting Started

IN THIS SECTION:

Adding a water garden to a home landscape can be a simple project of just a few steps or a more complicated one involving excavation and construction. However you approach your project, careful planning will help you avoid surprises and pitfalls along the way. On the following pages is an overview of the entire procedure that will help you assess your own outdoor needs before you launch into a water project.

Besides satisfying your own expectations for introducing water into the landscape, your plans should take into account your family's as well as your neighbors' safety and pleasure and any local or legal requirements. It also helps to anticipate what your situation will be a few years in the future, so your plans reflect permanence along with the possibility for change. The most important permanent features are location and materials, so included here are steps to help with site planning and construction. Whether you choose a shallow prefabricated pool or a more complicated larger pond, it will likely remain in place for years to come.

Of course, no water garden is complete without plants. In the pages that follow, you'll find tips on how to select and grow appropriate species and important information about how plants influence the ecology and maintenance of a pond.

Planning a Water Feature

Satisfying, successful water gardens and fountains begin with a vision. Imagine your water feature as completely as you can. Visit water gardens and look at photos in books and magazines for inspiration. Your climate and landscape style, municipal regulations, lifestyle, available time, and budget will influence your water garden's size, shape, materials, and equipment.

As you plan your water feature, let your home and landscape help decide its style. A geometrically shaped reflecting pool of cut stone complements formal landscapes, while an irregularly shaped pond with rocks, aquatic plants, and falling water suits a more casual home.

Climate plays a role in your choices, too. To keep fish outdoors year round, you'll need a minimum water depth and equipment to maintain water temperature. Seasonal rainfall may determine whether you install an overflow drain or automatic refill device.

Also consider your personal lifestyle. If you will view your garden mostly in the evening, install lighting or build the feature near a deck or patio. Short on time? Install a small container garden or build a large pond. Small ponds with fewer than 100 gallons of water require more work to maintain water quality. ❧

YOUR WATER GARDEN

If your plan includes plants and fish, design your pond to meet their needs. A pump to circulate and aerate the water and a filter to prevent water pollution are musts for most fishponds. The kinds of plants and animals that you want to include also dictate the depth, size, and style of your pond. Koi tend to damage water plants, many turtles eat fish, and water lilies resent splashing water, for example. Some plants need shallow water; others prefer deep water.

Municipal regulations and neighbors may also influence your water garden choices. Contact your municipal office for guidance on the size, depth, and placement of water features, outdoor plumbing, electrical fixtures, and required safety equipment. Before you finalize your plans, locate underground utilities and irrigation lines that could interfere with construction.

As you collect ideas and begin to design your water garden, list the materials you need. Pool liners, pumps, filters, and hired labor are usually the most expensive components. Rocks, lighting, and plants can also add up. If you need to hire an electrician, plumber, or excavator, find those with pond installation experience. 🌺

A SENSE OF SOUND. *Moving water adds the dimension of sound to the garden. Consider the look and sound you desire.*

CHOOSING THE RIGHT STYLE. *An informal water garden has an irregular edge, rather than the smooth lines of a formal pool.*

ADDING FISH. *Fish add color and movement but may require filtered water. Consider the kind and number of fish you want to stock.*

SAFER WATER GARDENS. *If you don't want open water, install a bubble fountain with inaccessible water reservoirs.*

Choosing a Location

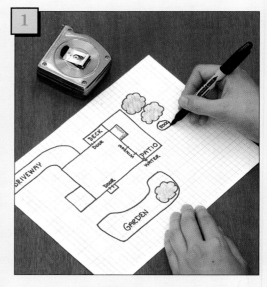

Using a tape measure and graph paper, measure and map your property, showing buildings, trees, pavement, and utilities.

The natural and man-made features of your site can enhance or limit the installation and enjoyment of your water garden. Careful planning and experimenting on paper can make your water garden safer, simpler, and easier to maintain.

First, make a map of your yard on graph paper, showing structures, pavement, property lines and setbacks, and buried utilities and irrigation pipes that can influence where you put your water garden. Also, mark the locations of convenient outside electric receptacles, faucets, and drains and, if possible, position your water feature near these existing services. Note trees on the map, because their roots may disrupt the pond liner, while falling leaves and twigs add to your maintenance chores.

Next, note the patterns of sun and shade. Water lilies and most other water plants need at least 6 hours of sun each day during the growing season. Also determine the places from which you will view the water feature. If you will see it from inside the house, look out the windows and choose a pond site with the view in mind. Passersby and visitors will enjoy a front yard pond if it is visible from the road or entrance to your property. Choose a more secluded spot if you want to enjoy your pond in private.

The size, shape, and slope of your site can be critical to your water garden's configuration and placement. Although a natural low spot may seem ideal for a water garden, it's usually unsuitable because surface water may undermine or dislodge the liner and overflow the pond. Slopes present another challenge, because pond edges must be level.

But consider your constraints and use them to your advantage. A narrow strip of land may become a stream. A slope can hold a waterfall or series of small, connected pools. A balcony can accommodate a fountain or a container of water plants. You can overcome even a poorly drained site by installing an aboveground water garden. ❧

HAVE ON HAND:

- Tape measure
- Graph paper and markers
- Tracing paper
- Shovel
- 2- to 3-foot-long wood stakes
- Mallet
- String
- Line level

A high water table can buckle pool liners. Dig a pond-depth test hole at the lowest point in your pond site, at the wettest time of year.

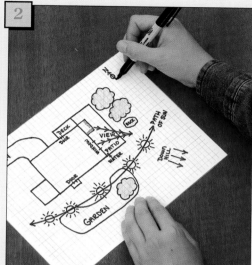

On the map, add observations about the site's sun and shade and drainage. Note views from house and other important vantage points.

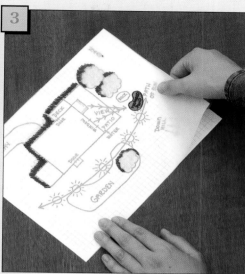

Draw the shape of your water feature on tracing paper. Then lay it over the map and move it around until you find the ideal spot.

Installed ponds must be level. Determine the slope of your pond site by driving pairs of stakes opposite each other around the perimeter.

Attach string tautly to pairs of stakes. Use a line level to adjust string until level. Measure heights of string at stakes to gauge difference.

HERE'S HOW
DESIGN TIPS

Choose a style that complements your existing landscape. Geometric shapes, bricks, and cut stone befit formal homes, while naturalistic ponds suit more casual landscapes.

Use a theme, such as attracting butterflies or creating a tropical oasis, to unify your design.

Repeat elements such as materials, colors, and shapes to connect the water garden to the site. Use similar stones or wood throughout your landscape and pond or echo the curve of the driveway with the pond edge.

Add mystery by revealing parts of the water garden from different vantage points. Disguise the sources of streams and waterfalls behind a curve, stone, or group of plants.

Vary shapes, textures, and colors. Use tall, medium, and low as well as spiky, soft, and rounded elements. Blend complementary flower colors and add plants with different-colored foliage for contrast or focal points.

Containers and Equipment

Nearly anything that holds water can contain a water garden. Half-barrels, tubs, and urns can hold a dwarf water lily, a bog garden, or a mix of aquatic plants, adding new dimensions to patios and porches. Bowls and ceramic pots fitted with submersible pumps make attractive fountains. Even old sinks, tubs, and livestock troughs can become water gardens when painted or disguised with a stonelike mix called hypertufa. In-ground water gardens typically use either rigid preformed liners or flexible pool liners to contain the water.

When you choose a container, look for one that holds enough water to support the plants and animals you want to keep in it. The container's depth and diameter matter, too. Deeper containers maintain a more stable temperature, which is important if you plan to add fish or put the container where daily temperatures fluctuate widely. Diameter is a factor, as the amount of surface area determines the rate of gas exchange and the number of fish and plants the container can support. If you plan to add a pump and fountain, be sure that the container holds enough water to keep the pump submerged without frequent refilling.

POOL LINERS

For larger water gardens, you can choose from preformed pond shells or flexible pool liners. Preformed shells, usually made from fiberglass, high-density polyethylene, or other rigid plastics, come in many shapes and sizes. Look for one with a minimum 18-inch depth; a strong, level, unwarped edge; and wide plant shelves.

Flexible pool liners let you choose the size and shape of your water garden. The best liner materials—EPDM and Butyl—are synthetic rubber, which makes them durable and easy to shape. They usually have 20-year warranties, as well as longer life expectancies, than other materials.

If space—or money—is an issue, a half whiskey barrel makes a very satisfactory water garden, especially if you are a beginner. ❧

HAVE ON HAND:

- Wooden half-barrel
- Duct tape
- Plumber's epoxy
- Flexible knife
- Waterproofing compound
- Paintbrush

TO WATERPROOF A BARREL, *cover large holes or gaps with duct tape on the outside of the container.*

From the inside, press plumber's epoxy into holes to seal. Let dry and cure for 24 hours. Once epoxy is cured, remove duct tape from the outside.

Seal with waterproofing compound on the inside of thoroughly dry container. Apply in a well-ventilated area and coat surface completely.

Allow the sealant to dry for 24 hours or per manufacturer's directions. Apply a second coat. Let dry thoroughly before testing for leaks.

PUMPS AND FILTERS

The first step in choosing the right pump is determining exactly what you want it to do. Decide whether it will power a fountain, filter, or waterfall. Measure the height of the water outlet above the top of the pump, known as the head, and the width and length of streams and waterfalls. Calculate the capacity of your reservoir pool.

Pump capacity is measured as the number of gallons per hour (GPH) that the pump can move at 1 foot above its outlet. Its capacity decreases as the head height increases. The length and diameter of the hose between the pump and its outlet affect capacity as well.

FILTER SYSTEM. *Submersible water pumps have a screened inlet to filter out debris, and an outlet pipe. Some models have a volume control.*

The width of the waterfall also determines the size pump you need. For flexibility, choose a pump that provides more capacity than you think you need. Use a flow restricter on the outlet hose to adjust volume, if necessary.

Keep your pump functioning efficiently and decrease maintenance by placing your pump in a filter box. The filter prevents debris from clogging the pump's inlet screen. In addition, filters can serve two other functions: mechanical and biological water purification. Mechanical filters simply remove particles from the water. Biological filters provide a medium in which beneficial, pollution-controlling bacteria thrive.

Larger ponds typically require an external filter that sits outside the pond. Water enters the filter box, either by gravity or through a pump, and then returns to the pond after filtering. Use the outlet from the filter to feed a waterfall or stream. You can also filter pond water through a small, plant-filled marsh. Water enters the marsh, where particles settle out and plants and bacteria use the nutrients for growth. The marsh should equal at least 10 percent of the pond area. ❧

HAVE ON HAND:

- Small submersible pump
- Small filter box
- Fountainhead
- Plastic storage box, 33 gallons or less, with lid
- Electric drill with ½-inch bit
- 1000 GPH or larger submersible pump
- Filter foam
- Bio-filter material
- Flexible hose to attach to pump outlet

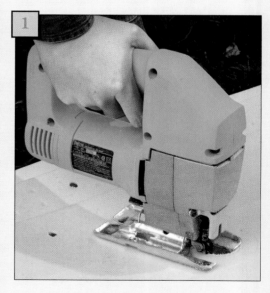

Make a filter for small ponds from a plastic storage box. Cut a hole for the pump outlet pipe in the lid, then drill ½-inch holes all over the lid.

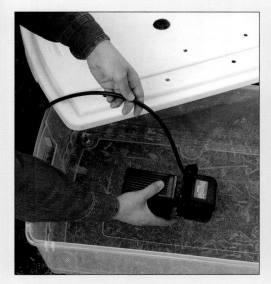

PUMP PROTECTION. *Putting pump in a filter box protects pump intake from clogging and helps clarify water biologically and mechanically.*

AERATION AND EFFECT. *Attach a fountainhead to outlet pipe of pump to aerate water and achieve a variety of decorative effects.*

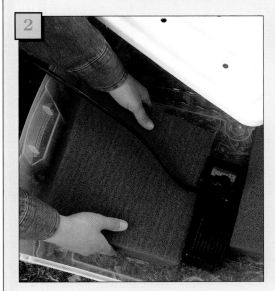

Set 1,000 GPH or larger pump in box and surround with a coil of filter foam. Fill box with filter media designed for biological filters.

Attach a flexible black pipe to pump outlet and run it to top of a waterfall or fountain. Submerge filter in the deepest part of pond.

HERE'S HOW
ELECTRICAL SAFETY

Water and electricity can add up to danger, but most water features need electrical service to operate pumps and lights. Safety precautions and planning can keep your water garden from causing electrical accidents.

Hire a licensed electrician to install weatherproof, outdoor-approved, ground fault circuit interrupter (GFCI) receptacles and connect them to a circuit breaker. Bury wires in a conduit to prevent digging accidents that may cut into the line. Place the receptacle away from areas of flooding and splashing water and protect it from mower and string trimmer damage. Never use extension cords, which may cause a serious shock if damaged or allowed to become wet.

Adding Low-Voltage Lighting

Subtle lighting adds mystery and elegance to your water garden and allows you to enjoy your garden in the evening. Low-voltage lights can highlight a fountain, waterfall or other special feature, illuminate the water from below the surface, or cast intriguing shadows over the pool.

Low-voltage systems use a transformer to change standard 120-volt household current to 12 volts, reducing risk of shock and increasing electrical safety outdoors and around water.

Transformers are usually rated from 100 to 600 watts—the higher the wattage rating, the more wires and fixtures it can service. Add up the total wattage for all the fixtures and bulbs you plan to install to find the size transformer you need. Mount the transformer next to the GFCI outlet receptacle and as close to the fixtures as possible.

A special low-voltage wire runs between the transformer and the lights. To determine the size wire you need, add up the wattage listed on the fixtures. Plan your layout so that no wire runs farther than 100 feet from the transformer. Avoid splicing wire, which can lead to water leaking into the joint, damage to the system, and electrical shock to humans or pets. ❧

LANDSCAPE LIGHTING

Fixture materials and styles range from inexpensive plastic to artistic brass and bronze. Unless the fixture is decorative, conceal it with plants or rocks so that only the light shows. Dark-colored fixtures blend into the landscape creating a more natural appearance. Regardless of the light style you choose, be sure to use only UL-listed fixtures to help ensure their safety. Attach fixtures to the wire according to the manufacturer's instructions. ❧

Mount weatherproof transformer next to outdoor-rated GFCI receptacle, as close as possible to light fixtures, according to manufacturer's advice.

Install light fixtures in or near pond, with none requiring more than 100 feet of wire to reach transformer. Disguise with plants and rocks.

Attach low-voltage wire to transformer per manufacturer's instructions. Run wire to each light fixture and attach fixtures.

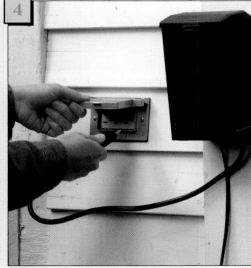

Plug the transformer into the receptacle and test the lights. Bury the wire 2 to 3 inches deep or leave on the ground.

HAVE ON HAND:

- ▶ Weatherproof low-voltage transformer
- ▶ Outdoor-rated GFCI receptacle
- ▶ Low-voltage light fixtures
- ▶ Low-voltage wire
- ▶ Screwdriver
- ▶ Underwater floodlights or spotlights
- ▶ Floating globe lights

TYPES OF LOW-VOLTAGE LIGHTING

You can choose from many styles of outdoor lighting. Some lights are designed for general use, while other fixtures are meant for use in and around water. Landscape lights illuminate paths and highlight special features. Lights may be submerged, floated, or mounted near water's edge. The secret to using landscape lighting is to use it subtly to enhance your yard and garden. Avoid adding too many lighting fixtures or colored lenses, which emphasize the lighting instead of the landscape.

Decide whether the light fixture will be an attractive garden feature, such as a bronze or copper lamp, or will be utilitarian and hidden among the foliage. The best quality landscape lights are made from copper, brass, and bronze, followed by aluminum and steel. Plastic is the least expensive but also the least durable.

More expensive fixtures usually have better quality interior parts, longer warranties, and lower maintenance requirements. Choose high-quality waterproof plastic fixtures for in-pool lighting. For fixtures that decorate the landscape by day and by night, select artistically designed copper, brass, or bronze fixtures. Use less expensive fixtures where they will be hidden by plants. Use only UL-listed materials.

Light fixtures and bulbs offer a wide range of effects. Upward pointing spotlights cast narrow beams of light, while floodlights illuminate wider areas. Use uplights to highlight branches, fountains, statues, or other features. Mount them on the ground or in the pond so that the fixture is hidden and only the light is revealed. Take care that lights do not shine in windows, paths, or roads, where the glare may disturb others.

Downlights shine on the ground, creating a subtle glow, especially when placed behind rocks and under foliage. Use these along paths for safety or mount them in trees to cast shadows on the ground. Avoid letting lights shine and create glare on the pond's surface.

Underwater and floating lights can illuminate pond water or shine on a moving water feature. Submerged lights are most effective in crystal clear water. Aim lights to point up into the spray of fountains or place them behind or under waterfalls. Anchor floating lights by setting a stone on the wire at the bottom of the pond. When lighting a pond containing fish, leave parts of the pool dark for the animals' comfort and turn off lights when you are through viewing the pool. ❀

FOR OVERALL LIGHTING. *Underwater floodlights illuminate the pool and create a glowing oasis in the darkness.*

FLOATING LIGHTS. *Globe lights can be anchored by placing a rock or brick on the cord at the bottom of the pool.*

FOR SPOTLIGHTING. *Underwater spot-light on waterfall highlights falling water.*

LIGHTING FOUNTAINS. *Special kits include underwater spotlights with a fountain combination for dramatic effects.*

LIGHTING FOCAL POINTS. *Poolside uplights highlight trees and shrubs. Take care not to create glare or shine lights toward neighbors.*

LIGHTING PATHWAYS. *Use poolside downlights to subtly illuminate paths and call attention to poolside gardens.*

HERE'S HOW

ABOUT LOW-VOLTAGE WIRE

Special low-voltage wire is sold in various sizes. Add up the wattage listed on the fixtures that you want to run to determine the size wire you need. For example, number 14 wire can handle up to 144 watts, number 12 wire takes up to 192 watts, and number 10 wire takes up to 288 watts. Plan your layout so that no wire runs more than 100 feet from the transformer, which is the maximum recommended length.

You can bury the wire 6 to 12 inches deep or leave it on top of the ground in places without foot or machine traffic. If you choose to leave wire on top of the ground, cover it with mulch to hide it from view and to prevent tripping. Choose wire with UV stabilized insulation, rated SPT 1, 2, or 3, for longest life. Place it in a conduit where it won't be damaged by mowers, edgers, or digging.

Choosing Water Plants

Plants bring your water garden to life. In addition to their beauty, water plants provide oxygen, shade, food, and habitat for fish. They form a critical link in healthy pond ecology by using up nutrients in the water and preventing excess algae. Water plants fall into three general categories—floating, submerged, and marsh or marginal.

Floating plants cover the water's surface. Some, such as water lettuce and duckweed, float freely on the water surface with their roots dangling below. Others, such as water lily and water poppy, root firmly in the bottom of the pond, but send leaves up to float on the surface. To shade your pond and sup-press algae growth, allow floating plants to cover 50 to 70 percent of the surface.

Submerged plants, also called oxygenating plants, live entirely or almost entirely under the water surface. They compete with algae for nutrients and provide oxygen and habitat for fish. Some, such as tape grass, root in the pond bottom or in pots containing soil. Others, such as hornwort, drift under the surface unless anchored in pots of smooth pea gravel. They have few roots and absorb nutrients directly through their leaves. Add one bunch of submerged plants per 1 to 2 square feet of pond surface to keep algae under control.

Marginal or marsh plants grow in the shallow water or moist soil near the water's edge. Some, such as cattails and sedges, grow upright, while others, like watercress and creeping Jennie, scramble along the bank and in shallow water. They soften the transition from water to land and help prevent raccoons and other fish predators from entering the pond.

Planting in pots simplifies maintenance. You can arrange plants easily and take them out of the pond for cleaning and winter storage. Although you can plant marsh plants directly in the soil, potting them prevents invasive species from overgrowing their boundaries. 🐾

HAVE ON HAND:

▶ Shallow 2- to 3-gallon nursery pots

▶ Newspaper

▶ Water plant fertilizer tablets

▶ Aquatic plant potting mix

▶ Umbrella palm division ready for potting

▶ ½-inch-diameter smooth pea gravel

SUBMERGED PLANTS. *Plants like anacharis remove excess nitrogen and add oxygen to water. Set stems in pots with pea gravel.*

PLANTING MARGINALS. *Cover holes of wide, shallow 2- to 3-gallon pot with 2 layers of damp newspaper. Place fertilizer tablets on bottom.*

FLOATING PLANTS. *These plants often have trailing roots that filter the water, colorful bloom, and leaves that shade the surface.*

MARGINAL PLANTS. *Use marsh plants like cattails along pond margins to add height, filter water, and set off other water plants.*

Fill with 5 to 6 inches of aquatic plant potting mix. Center plant in pot; work gently into soil until crown is just above surface.

To hold the soil in place, cover the surface with 1 to 2 inches of pea gravel, keeping it away from the plant crown.

HERE'S HOW
RESTRICTED PLANTS

Some aquatic and marsh plants have outgrown their welcome in many parts of the country. The U.S. Department of Agriculture and each state government maintain lists of restricted plants that they consider noxious weeds. These restricted species become invasive and threaten natural waterways and native plant communities.

The federal list of aquatic and wetland weeds currently contains about 20 species of plants, but state lists often contain many more plant species that may not be possessed, collected, transported, cultivated, or imported without a special license. Ethical mail-order nurseries will not knowingly ship any listed plants to those states that restrict them.

Find the federal list on the Web at: http://aquat1.ifas.ufl.edu/prohib.html or http://www.aphis.usda.gov./ppq/bats/fnwsbycate.html. Contact your state agencies for local restrictions.

Understanding Pond Ecology

Understanding the basics of how water plants, animals, microorganisms, and chemicals interact in the water is the key to a healthy, low-maintenance pond. Nitrogen and bacteria play the starring roles in the nitrogen cycle—a process that converts fish and plant waste into nutrients that water plants use for growth.

In the first stage of the nitrogen cycle, bacteria consume fish waste and decaying plant and animal matter and produce ammonia as a by-product. Another kind of bacterium turns ammonia into nitrites. Ammonia and nitrites are deadly to fish. A third bacterium, however, uses oxygen to turn the nitrites into nitrates, which are beneficial plant nutrients relatively harmless to fish. A balanced system occurs when enough plants exist to absorb the nutrients and enough pond bacteria are present to safely decompose the amount of waste that the plants and animals produce.

You can monitor the levels of ammonia, nitrites, and nitrates in your pond with test kits. Many shops will also test your water for a small fee. Chemical additives can help balance the water chemistry, but establishing a natural equilibrium requires less maintenance in the long run. Newly established ponds may take several weeks or longer to achieve balance.

Oxygen also plays a critical role in pond ecology. Some bacteria produce toxic gases, such as carbon dioxide, methane, hydrogen sulfide, and ammonia, when they live in oxygen-deprived environments. Aerating your water feature with a fountain or waterfall and circulating the water throughout the pond will reduce the amount of these harmful chemicals by increasing the level of oxygen in the water.

The amount of water surface area exposed to the air is also important, especially in small water gardens and containers. Water temperature affects the efficiency of the nitrogen cycle and the comfort of the pond inhabitants, too. Very hot or cold water inhibits bacteria growth and function. Warm water also contains less oxygen than cool water.

In addition to natural water chemicals, most municipal water supplies contain chlorine, and often chloramine, to kill harmful microorganisms. Chloramine is a chemical made of chlorine and ammonia, both of which are toxic to fish. Chlorine dissipates when exposed to air, but chloramine does not. It requires neutralizing with a chemical that is readily available at pet stores.

Use floating plants to cover 50 to 70 percent of the water surface to block the sunlight, which algae needs to grow.

Install a filter to remove particles that cloud the water and to improve beneficial bacteria growth.

Add one bunch of submerged water plants per 1 to 2 square feet of water surface to compete with and starve the algae.

Aerate the water with a fountain spray or waterfall to increase oxygen, reduce toxic gases, and promote the growth of beneficial bacteria.

Add fish to control mosquitoes and provide nutrients for lush plant growth.

Skim fallen leaves and other debris from the pond, especially in the fall, to prevent the decaying foliage from polluting the water.

HERE'S HOW
ALGAE BLOOMS

Algae blooms are excessive algae growths that cloud the water or cover the pond with a blanket of green. They often occur in newly established ponds and in the spring before the pond plants grow large enough to compete for nutrients and light. Algae blooms signal the presence of too much sunlight or too many nutrients such as nitrogen and phosphorus.

Although algae blooms will usually clear up on their own when you have enough water plants to successfully compete, you can prevent and control blooms using several methods. Add blue or black pond dye to shade the water temporarily. Set submerged plants close to the surface, where they can receive adequate light.

Vacuum or scoop sediment from the pond bottom to remove the source of nutrients. Avoid overfeeding fish and overfertilizing plants. Add one bunch of submerged, oxygenating plants per square foot of pond surface area to consume the available nutrients.

Maintaining Ponds and Fountains

Keeping pond water clear, pumps and filters running efficiently, and plants and fish healthy is the goal of routine maintenance. Regular summer care takes as little as a few minutes a week for small tubs to as much as an hour for large ponds. Preparing the pond for winter and starting it up again in cold climates takes a little longer, but overall, water gardens need little attention.

Summer maintenance consists of feeding the fish daily and skimming debris and leaves from the pond. Once a week or whenever needed, check the pump, filters, and fountain for clogging. Rinse out sponge filters with pond water, not chlorinated tap water, and clear leaves and other debris from the intake vents. If fountainheads become plugged, clean them with a pipe cleaner and vinegar to remove mineral deposits. Add water to the pond as needed and check water chemistry every week or so, especially in the spring and after adding fish, to be sure that toxic waste is not building up. Fertilize the plants once a month by pushing an aquatic plant fertilizer tablet into the soil near plant roots. Remove long strands of blanket algae by scooping them out or winding them on a stick.

In climates with freezing winter temperatures, autumn chores include draining the plumbing and removing pumps, filters, and tender plants for storage. If fish will remain in the pond, siphon the muck from the bottom if deeper than 1 inch, and change 25 to 30 percent of the pond water. To allow toxic gases to escape, keep a hole in the ice open with a pond heater, but do not keep a pump running. Stop feeding fish when the water temperature drops below 50°F. Skim fallen leaves from the pond or stretch a net above the surface to catch them.

In spring, set up the pump and filter after hard freezes have ended. Divide and repot overwintering plants, and add one bunch of submerged plants per 1 to 2 square feet of surface area. Prevent algae bloom by adding pond-shading dye to the water or covering about 60 percent of the surface with plants. ❦

HAVE ON HAND:

- ► Buckets
- ► Garden hose
- ► Pond vacuum
- ► Wooden or plastic spoon
- ► Plastic dustpan
- ► Soft broom or rags
- ► Pond net or skimmer net

Reserve some bacteria-laden pond water in buckets to add back to the pond to help restart the biological activity.

Scoop out muck with a wooden or plastic tool and place it in a bucket. Take care not to damage pond liner.

Carefully remove all fish and plants from the pond and place them in the reserved water. Place buckets in a shady place.

Siphon water from bottom of pond through a garden hose with attached pond vacuum device.

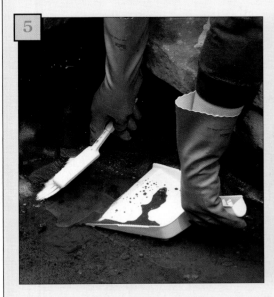

Carefully clean most of muck off liner with soft broom or rag. Leave algae on sides to help restart biological activity.

PUMP CARE. Throughout the summer, clean the pump intake and filters each week, or as needed, to remove debris and prevent clogging.

HERE'S HOW
STORING WATER LILIES

Hardy water lilies can remain in ponds that do not freeze solid to the bottom, but must be removed and stored if grown in tubs and container gardens. Tropical water lilies should not be subjected to temperatures below 50°F.

Store water lilies in one of several ways. One method is to remove plants from their pots, hose off the soil, and trim the leaves and roots. Place the fleshy rhizomes in bags of slightly damp sand or sphagnum moss and store at 50° to 55°F. Alternatively, leave hardy water lilies in their pots and seal them in plastic bags in a cool, but not freezing, place.

Water lilies can also be grown through the winter in a greenhouse or under fluorescent grow lights in tubs. Give them full sun or 14 to 16 hours of light per day.

Building Basics

Once you've made the decision to build a water garden and have selected its site, the next step is to determine its size and shape. Before you settle on a design, it's worthwhile making a critical assessment of your landscape. You'll want to take advantage of its visual and physical strengths, such as natural changes in elevation and existing vegetation. On the other hand, physical barriers such as rock or hardpan and tree roots may limit the possibilities.

Whatever type of water garden you choose, strive to integrate it stylistically into other areas of your garden so that it blends harmoniously with its surroundings. Aboveground pools have the limitation of appearing unnatural, but they are among the most artistic of landscape features. In this section, you will see how to build one from scratch out of wood, as well as how to make your own "antique" faux-stone water garden container. In a formal landscape, a circular water garden of concrete or tile may be more suitable. If your site invites an in-ground pool, you have the option of installing either a flexible or a preformed liner. Flexible liners allow for a limitless number of shapes, while the preformed ones speed up the installation process.

When you're ready for the finishing touches to your construction project, you'll see how to line the edges with stones and other materials for various garden styles. ❧

An Aboveground Water Garden

Building a pool above ground brings the water garden closer to hand and eye level for easy viewing and maintenance, and it eliminates the need to dig a large hole. Raised water features are also safer if you have children and pets, and they are less attractive to fish predators. Aboveground pools are ideal for yards with a high water table, seasonal flooding, or soil that's difficult to work.

To build a water garden, use materials that match the style of your landscape. Landscape timbers—either natural wood or plastic wood—a blend of recycled plastic and wood, make a quick and easy informal pool. Pressure-treated lumber can be used if the wood does not come in contact with the water in the garden. Let the materials and landscape and your building expertise suggest the water garden's shape, too—from square or rectangular to multisided.

Water and marginal plants placed in the pool and around the perimeter add height, soften the edges, and blend the pool into the landscape. Set a spouting fountain on the edge of the pool, or build a low waterfall or weir to return water from a submerged filter and pump.

A WOOD-SIDED POOL

Build an aboveground water garden from stacked landscape timbers. Smooth, level, and firmly pack the soil on the site. Then spread a 2- to 4-inch-deep layer of sand as a cushion for the liner and landscape timbers. Line the timber box with a flexible pool liner. Fill the liner with water to settle it before sandwiching it between the top timber and the ledge board. Add a wide ledge around the top perimeter for sitting and placing potted plants. 🌸

HAVE ON HAND:

- Rake
- Sand
- Landscape timbers, 4 x 4 or 5 x 5 by 8 feet long
- Circular saw
- Hammer and chisel
- 6-inch spikes
- Electric drill with bits
- ⅜-inch rebar (#3)

- Hand sledge
- Flexible pool liner
- Scissors
- Staple gun and staples
- 1- x 8-inch cedar decking, for seat around top
- Galvanized screws 3½ inches long

Determine site and dimensions of pool. Excavate area and rake level. Spread a 2-inch-thick layer of sand over area, and smooth.

Measure and cut timbers to desired length. Use a circular saw to cut lap joints at ends of all of the timbers.

Finish lap joints by breaking off the rough pieces with a hammer and chisel.

Lay out frame two timbers high, fitting lap joints together at corners. Use 6-inch spikes to hold in place. Place another set of timbers on first two.

To use rebar to anchor frame to ground, drill holes at corners of frame with wood bit sized slightly smaller in diameter than rebar.

Cut four sections of rebar 8 inches longer than height of pool. Use a hand sledge to hammer rebar through predrilled holes at corners.

Cut flexible liner to size, allowing a 4- to 5-inch overlap at top. Lay in pool, partially fill with water, and staple liner over top timbers.

For seating around edge, cut 1- x 8-inch cedar decking to fit, mitering corners. Screw decking in place with 3½-inch screws. Fill pool.

HERE'S HOW

NEUTRALIZING CONCRETE

Lime used in concrete mixes can leach into the pool water and kill fish and plants by raising the pH of the water. You can counteract the lime by rinsing the cured concrete with vinegar. Add 1 gallon of vinegar for every 100 gallons of water. Rinse well. Repeat the process if the pool water pH remains high.

Waterproofing compounds that seal the concrete also prevent lime from leaching into the water. Before applying either rubber-base paint or epoxy, etch and clean the concrete by scrubbing it with 1 part hydrochloric acid (formerly called muriatic acid) diluted with 2 parts water. Wear protective gloves, glasses, and clothing to prevent contact with the acid. Rinse thoroughly and dispose of water where it cannot harm plants, lawn, or pets.

Alternatives

WATER GARDEN IN A HALF-BARREL

You can make a small raised or buried water garden from a decay-resistant oak half-barrel. These small, easy-to-install features blend into the garden while allowing you to grow plants that require very different soil and moisture levels. Water temperatures remain more stable in a partially buried barrel than one completely above ground.

Line the barrel with a piece of flexible pool liner or a preformed rigid liner, available from garden centers and pond supply stores. If you use a flexible liner, secure it with wood lath strips placed over the liner just inside the lip of the barrel. Use galvanized screws to hold them in place. Partially fill with water to adjust liner before securing it.

If you wish to bury the barrel, measure the diameter of the barrel at the desired depth and dig a hole to fit. Choose a spot that receives at least 6 hours of sun per day if you want to grow a dwarf water lily, lotus, or other sun-loving plant. Fill the barrel with water or soil, depending on the plants you want to grow. Good choices for a semiraised barrel include bog and marsh plants, such as pitcher plants and sundews, cattails, arrowhead, and papyrus, or small water plants. ❧

BRICK-VENEERED WATER GARDEN

In a formal landscape where space does not allow for a long, low reflecting pool, a raised water feature veneered with brick is a good solution. A brick exterior provides neatness and formality that dresses up a garden setting, whereas wood planks and timbers lend a sense of rustic naturalism.

During construction, provide for all plumbing and electrical lines needed, with possibilities for future expansion, such as lighting and a fountain. Build an inner wall out of poured concrete or blocks. To prevent settling and cracking, especially in unstable soils, begin with a firm and level concrete footing 4 inches deep and one-and-a-half times wider than the finished wall. Be sure to reinforce the concrete pad with wire mesh or rebar. Set additional rebar rods at the corners to tie the wall to the pad. Cover the exterior with mortared brick and seal the interior with waterproofing compound.

Formal ponds generally feature few plant species, but water lilies never fail to add a regal tone. If your design includes a fountain, plan on a very gentle spray. Water lilies grow best in undisturbed water. ❧

Installing a Flexible Pool Liner

Sheets of flexible pool liner let you create any size or shape pond that you can imagine. You can install them in a soil-lined hole, use them to waterproof a leaky concrete pond, or line an above-ground water garden. For durability and longest life, choose one made of Butyl or EPDM rubber. Avoid using swimming pool liners, roofing membrane, and plastic sheeting.

Before purchasing the liner, plan your design and layout on paper. Buy the liner after excavating the hole, so you can measure the size accurately. Allow at least 12 inches of extra material to overhang the perimeter.

Decide whether you want straight sides or plant shelves. Straight sides are easier to install and foil fish predators, but make working in the pond difficult. Make plant shelves at 12-inch levels from top to bottom and wide enough to support clusters of potted plants. After digging, compact the soil firmly or, in loose soil, pour concrete edges to prevent plant shelves and liner from settling. Consider digging an extra-deep section to hold a sump pump, which will make draining the pond easier in the future. Before installing the liner, line the entire excavation with cushioning fabric underlayment to prevent punctures. 🍂

LINING AN IN-GROUND POOL

Plan and mark the locations of your filter, plant shelves, waterfall, skimmer, and other built-in pond features before you dig. Use a carpenter's level on a long, straight board to check the perimeter and shelf levels and heights of important features.

Pool liners are heavy and may take several people to install. Liners become more flexible when warmed in the sun, but can kill grass underneath if allowed to become too hot. 🌿

HAVE ON HAND:

- Rope to mark perimeter
- Spray paint
- Shovel or spade
- Board that spans length of pond
- Carpenter's level
- Tape measure
- Tarps
- Garden rake
- Broom
- Fabric underlayment
- Flexible pool liner
- Garden hose and water source
- Stones

Outline pond area with rope. Adjust perimeter in wide, natural curves. View from all angles to get a pleasing shape. Mark with spray paint.

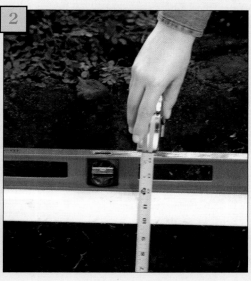

Excavate the hole to the depth of the first plant shelf. Use a board, carpenter's level, and tape measure to determine depth of shelf.

Use excavated soil to level edges of pond and pile excess on tarps. Create wide, natural berms. Check level in all directions as you work.

Mark outline of shelves with spray paint. Continue excavating until you reach desired depth of pond bottom. Check level.

Remove stones and roots from bottom, shelves, and sides. Sweep excavation with a broom until the surface is smooth.

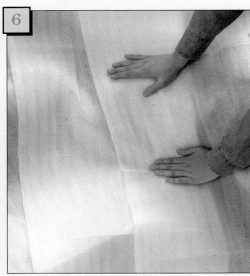

Install fabric underlayment over sides, shelves, and bottom. Pat into place with hands.

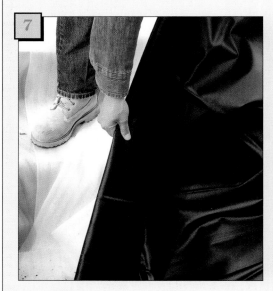

Install flexible pool liner, starting from center and working outward. Overlap pond perimeter by at least a foot; pleat for curves.

Be sure pond edge is level, then fill slowly with water; continue adjusting liner as needed. Secure with stones. See pages 40–43 to finish.

HERE'S HOW

DIGGING SAFETY

Consider underground electric, telephone, cable TV, water, or gas lines before you dig. Accidentally cutting into a gas or electrical line can be fatal. Damaging lines can also carry fines and penalties. Contact the local utility companies to have them mark the locations of their buried lines.

Sprinkler systems may also need to be moved before pond installation. Use spray paint to mark buried irrigation pipes and sprinkler heads and work around them or reconfigure the system around your pond. Locate ponds away from septic systems and leach fields.

Contact municipal offices before installing a water feature. Many towns regulate pool size, depth, placement, and safety precautions.

Alternatives

A STANDING POOL

You can build an aboveground water garden in nearly any size and shape, but a symmetrical rectangular pool is by far the easiest to assemble. One of the easiest and quickest construction methods is to build a simple wood frame fitted with a flexible pool liner. Wood is fairly inexpensive and goes up fast. Stained or painted to match your house or deck, wood will resist weathering for many years. Decorative trim along the top edges also functions as casual seating and space for displaying potted plants.

An advantage of a wood-frame, aboveground pool is its temporary nature. You can dismantle it at any time if you need the space for other uses. Whereas concrete and stone are more permanent, the flexible liner and wood shell are as easy to disassemble as they are to install.

When constructing the wood frame, prepare a secure footing and use strong materials to stabilize the walls. Install ample vertical support at corners and along the sides for horizontal lumber. Use construction lumber for the finished sides, or face it with another, more decorative wood. Line the shell with a fabric underlayment, and cover it with the flexible liner.

A BOG GARDEN

A true bog accumulates over many centuries, but you can create a small bog garden relatively quickly by following the same procedure you would to install a pond. For optimum plant health, make your bog garden at least 10 square feet in area and fit it with an overflow drain to prevent flooding.

A bog requires only a shallow 12-inch depression covered with a flexible pool liner. Instead of water, fill the liner with 6 inches of coarse silica quartz sand topped with 6 inches of thoroughly moistened sphagnum peat moss, which can be purchased in bales. To give your bog a natural character, add a final layer of green, living sphagnum moss. Press the strands well into the moist brown moss to ensure good contact with the growing medium.

The bog garden is a perfect site for moss, cranberry, and carnivorous plants, but you can add many moisture-loving ornamentals, too. Labrador tea, marsh marigold, water arum, globeflower, Japanese iris, and cardinal flower are just a few of the possibilities. In warm climates, papyrus and taro may be planted. To maintain the bog, keep it moist, but with no standing water. Every few years, add more brown moss to the lower layer.

A Preformed In-Ground Pond

Available in a wide range of shapes and sizes, preformed ponds offer many first-time water gardeners the confidence to begin their new hobby. Although not as simple to install as a flexible liner, preformed ponds are used to feature fountains or plants. To make a larger impact, connect two ponds with a stream or waterfall.

Less expensive plastic shells are available at home and garden centers. Pond supply stores also sell more durable and easy-to-repair fiberglass ponds. When shopping for a preformed pond, arrange some potted plants in and around various units to be sure that the size and shape will meet your needs. When in doubt, always choose the larger unit, because most pond owners eventually wish for a larger pond to accommodate their growing water plant and fish collections. If you plan to add fish, choose a pond that's at least 18 inches deep—water temperature fluctuates too widely in shallower ponds.

Preformed ponds require more exacting excavation than ponds with flexible liners—the more complicated the shape, the more difficult the job. Choose one with straight sides and a simple shape for easiest installation.

INSTALLING A PREFORMED POND

Getting the top of the unit level and supporting all parts of it with firmly packed soil are the two most critically important steps in the installation of preformed ponds. Check the level frequently and make adjustments as you dig and fill around the pond site. The pool lip should be an inch or two above ground level to prevent surface water from running into the finished pond. ❦

HAVE ON HAND:

- Preformed pond unit
- Bricks
- Carpenter's level
- 12 to 18 bamboo stakes
- Tape measure
- Rope
- Shovel or spade
- Board that spans length of pool
- Sand to cover bottom to a 2-inch depth
- Garden hose, water source
- Trowel

Set unit on ground in desired position. Support on bricks to hold it in place; adjust until level. Use bamboo stakes to mark perimeter.

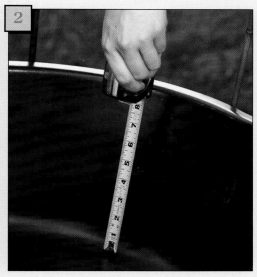

Measure height from first plant shelf to lip. Use rope to mark a line 4 inches outside staked perimeter. Excavate inside rope to depth of shelf.

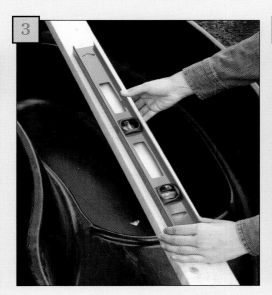

Set unit in hole and check its level across width and length with carpenter's level. Adjust soil depth as necessary.

Mark perimeter of deep part of pond with rope. Measure depth from shelf to pond bottom and excavate to 2 inches deeper than that depth.

Position unit in hole and check levels as before. Make adjustments in soil depth so that lip is 2 inches above ground level.

Remove any stones, sticks, or sharp objects from the hole. Spread a 2-inch layer of sand in the deep part of the hole to cushion the pond.

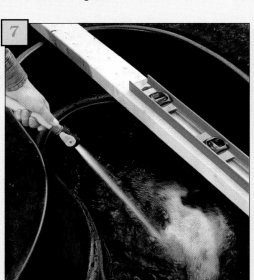

Position pond in the hole, fitting it snugly against the shelf and bottom. Check levels and adjust. Add 4 inches of water to pond to settle it.

Backfill firmly with sand or soil free of sharp debris. Gradually fill pond to within 2 to 3 inches of top as you backfill; check levels frequently.

HERE'S HOW

CALCULATING CAPACITY

Your pond's capacity determines the necessary pump and filter sizes, the dosage of water treatment chemicals, and the number of fish you can maintain. Measure the size of your pond in feet and use the following formulas to find the number of gallons it holds.

For a square or rectangular pond: Length × width × depth × 7.5 gallons = gallons in the pond.

For round ponds, find the radius, which is half the pond width, and calculate: radius × radius × 3.14 x depth × 7.5 gallons = gallons in the pond.

Calculate the volume of irregularly shaped ponds by dividing the pond into approximately rectangular and circular shapes. Calculate the volumes separately and then add them together. For ponds with plant shelves, calculate each layer separately.

Alternatives

AN ENCLOSED TUB

Preformed pools are designed for use in belowground pools. But with a few touches, small unadorned ones can be adapted to function above ground. To obscure the unattractive sides from view, surround the unit with a material compatible with your garden style.

In a woodland or country setting, consider using flexible strips of log edging around a low pool. For containers deeper than 12 inches, substitute individual posts driven into the ground around the circumference. Treated wood is most weather resistant, but any wood such as cedar, redwood, or locust that is suitable for outdoor use will do. Set the posts at uneven heights for added interest. In a more urban setting, consider a simple wood frame coated with stucco or a mosaic tile exterior, depending on the construction details in your garden and outdoor living area.

Small plants generally go in small water gardens, but there is nothing wrong with adding a large plant for drama if you are careful to divide it annually to restrain its growth. Try a graceful dwarf papyrus or spiky cattail for height and a day- or night-blooming tropical water lily for floral fragrance. 🌺

POND IN A TROUGH

Rigid forms make it easy to install a water garden either below or above the ground. Preformed fiberglass and plastic units are convenient, but usually too unattractive to use above ground. A more pleasing possibility is a freestanding agricultural tub or trough made out of corrugated galvanized steel. Outfitted with pond plants and dressed up with a sculpted fountain, this utilitarian container becomes a delightful pool and a tranquil resting spot in a cottage garden or a *potager*. As an aboveground pool, it assures high visibility and safety that are especially valuable in gardens frequented by children.

By placing a few submerged and floating plants inside the trough, you will give it the unmistakable look of a garden pool. Accompanied by a decorative skirt of well-placed plant companions, a metal trough quickly loses its original identity. You may also want to consider applying metallic or other ornamental trims to the exterior. Left plain, a trough gives a sleek, contemporary look. An option to the large, single, garden trough is a grouping of two or three smaller ones of differing heights connected with fountain spouts. 🌺

Creating a Naturalistic Edge

The transition from water to land occurs at the edge of your pond. The edging material you choose, whether natural stone, brick, or wood, is an integral part of the design and style of your water garden. Formal pools have sharp edges, usually made from bricks, flagstones, pavers, or concrete. Informal water features imitate natural ponds with a more gradual transition from water to shore and are often edged with marsh plants, gravel, and stones.

In most pond constructions, a firm foundation of compacted soil or concrete surrounds the pool and is covered with a fabric underlayment. The pond liner is then sandwiched between the underlayment and edging stones. The foundation keeps the pond edge stable and level and supports the weight of people and maintenance equipment. In climates with freezing winters, use foundation materials that won't crack or frost heave, such as compacted crushed stone.

To prevent the edging stones from shifting, seal them to the liner with spray polyfoam or concrete. If you place large boulders on the edge of the liner, pour a concrete foundation for them and install the liner over the concrete. Prevent liner damage by cushioning the boulders on a piece of fabric underlayment.

EDGING A POND WITH STONE

When you trim your pond liner during installation, allow at least 12 inches to extend beyond the pond edges. Seal it under the edging stones above the water level to prevent leaks. Edging stones usually overhang the pond edge by 1 to 2 inches to hide the liner and protect it from damaging sunlight. Tip the stones slightly so that rainwater flows away from the pond. ❧

HAVE ON HAND:

- ▶ Flagstones
- ▶ Eye protectors
- ▶ Stone chisel
- ▶ Mallet, 3 to 5 pounds
- ▶ Metal pipe or heavy board
- ▶ Premixed concrete mortar
- ▶ Hoe
- ▶ Wheelbarrow
- ▶ Concrete trowel
- ▶ Carpenter's level
- ▶ Jointing tool
- ▶ Water source
- ▶ Plastic sheeting

Fill pond and adjust liner; trim liner to extend at least 12 inches beyond pond edge. Leave extra at any waterfall or skimmer installations.

Arrange stones so they overhang pond edge by 2 inches and completely cover liner. Tip them slightly so rainwater drains away from pond.

Cut flagstones to fit, if necessary. Wear eye protection. Set stone on bed of sand or soft soil. Score cutting line with chisel and mallet.

Place a metal pipe or board under the stone along the cutting line. Strike along the line sharply with the chisel and hammer to break the stone.

To prevent stones from moving and to keep pond edge level, set stones in concrete mortar. Blend premixed mortar with water in a wheelbarrow.

Spread a 1-inch-thick layer of mortar on liner under each stone. Press stones into it, leaving gaps between them. Keep mortar out of water.

Check level around pond edge as you work. Let mortar dry for 24 hours. Pack mortar into gaps between stones; smooth with jointing tool.

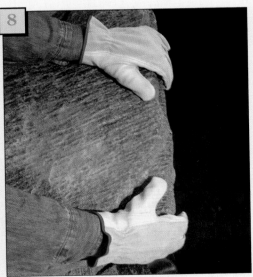

Keep mortar moistened or covered with plastic sheeting for 3 to 7 days to cure. Lay another course of stones on top to hide mortar.

HERE'S HOW

MOVING HEAVY STONES

Large stones and boulders add drama and give ponds a natural and finished appearance. But rocks weighing more than 50 to 100 pounds require care in lifting and moving into place. Bend your knees and face your load squarely, keep your back straight, and don't lift from a bent-over position. If possible, avoid lifting stones and use other methods to move them instead.

Drag smaller rocks on a heavy-duty tarp, moving only a few at a time. Tip large flat stones end over end. Use an iron pry bar as a lever by placing it between a smaller rock and a large boulder. Move large stones with a come-along, but pad and protect the trunks of trees, if used as anchors.

Alternatives

STEPPINGSTONES ACROSS A POND

Steppingstones invite exploration and ease pond maintenance. For safe and comfortable walking, choose some flat-topped stones, 18 inches or wider, and space them about 12 to 15 inches apart. Plan their placement before installing your pool liner.

Choose stones with a rough texture to prevent slipping. Irregular shapes suit informal ponds, while geometric squares and rounds fit into formal landscapes. For a more natural appearance, stagger the stones instead of placing them in a straight line.

After excavating your pond, pour concrete pads to support the foundations on which you will place the steppingstones. Pads should be at least 4 inches thick and poured over a layer of crushed stone. Dig below the bottom of the pond to the necessary depth, so that the top of each pad will be level with the pond bottom. After the concrete has cured, cover the pond with fabric underlayment and flexible pool liner. Build a support for each steppingstone on top of the pads, using concrete and bricks or concrete blocks. Use a carpenter's level and tape measure to be sure that each stone is level and will be above the final water surface. Mortar the stones in place. ❧

EDGING A POND WITH BRICK

An edge of straight lines and sharp angles around a garden pool lends a note of elegance and formality. Brick adds a special character and warmth that is lacking in concrete or stone, yet it provides the same permanent solidity that stays neatly in place and withstands the rigors of harsh climates. Freezing and thawing or heavy rains won't dislodge mortared brick, nor will soil from around pond margins ever erode into the water.

Although some brick projects are complex, a small project is easy enough to do yourself. Lay the brick on top of a concrete pad poured over a section of the flexible pool liner. Do this by excavating a shelf around the outside of your pond about 4 inches deep and as wide as your bricks are long. The shelf depth should correspond to half the thickness of the concrete foundation. The top of the concrete should be just above the level of the ground, and the inside plumb with the sides of the pool. When you line the pond, allow extra material to cover the shelf and another 12-inch overlap to bring up behind and slightly over the top of the concrete so the edge of the liner will remain above water level. Backfill all around with soil. ❧

Making a Faux-Stone Container

Antique stone sinks or troughs make ideal miniature water gardens for bog and small marsh plants, but they are difficult to find and expensive to buy. You can build your own stone trough from a cement and peat moss mix called hypertufa, or coat an existing glazed sink or tub to resemble stone.

Making a trough requires only simple tools and materials. You can design any shape or size container to fit your space or needs. Cardboard boxes make ideal forms to hold the wet mixture, but you can make a mold from wood or any other supportive material. You will need to peel the mold away from the hardened trough. Line the mold with plastic to ease the trough's removal. Hypertufa takes at least 1 to 2 weeks to dry before it's strong enough to use, so plan your project in advance.

If you use hypertufa mix to coat a glazed sink or tub, roughen the sides with an emery cloth and apply a bonding agent, which is available from hardware stores. Apply the mix to the outside and top edges of the sink, but not the inside. Paint the interior with black rubberized paint if you plan to use it for water plants, or leave it natural if planting a miniature marsh. 🌺

WORKING WITH HYPERTUFA

Create a natural-looking stone trough from Portland cement, sand, and peat moss. Add a concrete colorant to the mixture to complement your landscape, if you wish. For a natural look, encourage moss to grow on the outside of the trough. Add small stones or gravel to the mix for a rougher finish. 🌸

HAVE ON HAND:

- ▶ Two plastic storage boxes, one to fit inside the other, 2–3 inches smaller all around
- ▶ Heavy plastic sheeting
- ▶ Rubber gloves
- ▶ Wheelbarrow or plastic tub
- ▶ Portland cement
- ▶ Sand
- ▶ Screened peat moss
- ▶ Concrete colorant (optional)
- ▶ Water
- ▶ Hoe
- ▶ Masonry sealer and paintbrush
- ▶ Wire brush
- ▶ Papyrus, cattail, and water hyacinth

Line the inside of the larger plastic storage box with plastic sheeting. Smooth wrinkles; creases will show once trough is unmolded.

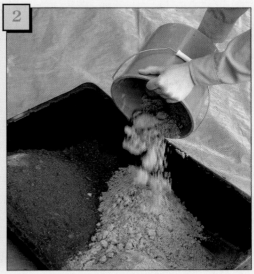

In a wheelbarrow or plastic tub, mix 1 part Portland cement, 1 part sand, and 2 parts screened peat moss.

Gradually add water to the dry ingredients, and combine with a hoe until the mix is evenly moist but still quite stiff.

Press a 2-inch-deep layer of mix into bottom of lined box. Center smaller box on the layer of mix.

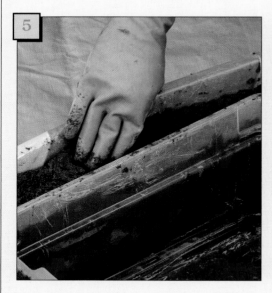

Pack mix into space between boxes, gently pressing out any air pockets. Cover boxes completely with plastic sheeting.

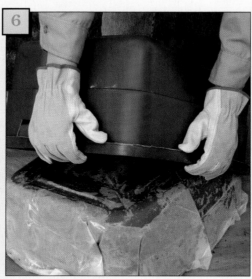

After 48 hours, remove plastic sheeting and lift out smaller box. Turn large box upside down, and remove trough. Let it sit to cure for 2 weeks.

Coat inside of trough with waterproof masonry sealer, according to manufacturer's directions. Rough sides with wire brush, if desired.

Fill trough with water. Place pots of papyrus and cattails in trough with soil level 2 to 4 inches below water level. Float hyacinth on surface.

HERE'S HOW

GROWING MOSS

Create an authentic-looking antique stone trough by encouraging moss to grow on its sides. Most mosses prefer acidic soil or growing medium. If coating a hypertufa container or one made of concrete, first neutralize the alkaline lime in the cement by washing it with ¼ cup of white vinegar mixed into a gallon of water. Rinse well.

To encourage moss, combine ½ cup of buttermilk and 1 quart of water in a blender; add bits of fine, live, green moss. Purée briefly to pulverize the moss. Paint or spray the mixture on the outside of the trough. Keep lightly moist until the moss sprouts and grows vigorously. Keep moist after the moss becomes established, never letting it completely dry out. Spring and other damp seasons are the best times to establish a moss-covered trough.

Alternatives

PLANTS FOR A TROUGH GARDEN

The best plants for trough gardens stay naturally small or are easy to manage and enjoy damp soil or an aquatic environment. When choosing plants, look for a mix of shapes, colors, and growing habits. For damp-soil gardens, choose tall, spiky horsetails or rushes to add height to the container. Creeping Jennie spreads its round leaves over the soil and hides the pot edge. Chameleon plant, marsh marigold, and other flowering plants provide colorful foliage and blooms. Plant directly into the soil and keep it wet, but don't let water cover the soil at all times.

For shallow water gardens, you can either plant directly into soil in the trough or put plants into individual pots. Use floating water lettuce, duckweed, or salvinia to cover the surface. Let water poppy trail over the sides and add dwarf cattail, water clover, or papyrus for height.

Give plants at least 6 hours of sun each day. You can move your trough garden indoors for the winter. Most water and marsh plants will survive in a 55° to 70°F room under grow lights. Leave the lights on for 12 hours a day.

PERENNIAL RICE
Zizania latifolia
10–12 feet tall
Zones 5–11
Marginal plant related to wild rice with flat, grassy leaves and slender, very tall, reedy stems. Feathery spikes of flowers appear in summer in warmer parts of range; full sun; sodden soil or shallows; spreads quickly once established.

CHAMELEON PLANT
Houttuynia cordata **'Variegata'**
6–12 inches tall
Zones 6–11
Heart-shaped leaves spattered with green, yellow, and red; small, white flowers in summer; spreads rapidly by runners; useful ground cover for moist soil and in water up to 3 inches deep; full sun to light shade.

WATER LETTUCE
Pistia stratiotes
2–4 inches tall
Zones 10–11
Floating aquatic plant with bowl-shaped rosette of evergreen, wavy leaves; small, tubular flowers in summer; full sun with some noon shade; keep water temperature 60 to 75°F; lift before first frost and overwinter in aquarium.

DWARF SWEET FLAG
Acorus gramineus **'Variegatus'**
8–12 inches tall
Zones 6–11
Bright green, irislike leaves striped with white or yellow; grows from a creeping rhizome that may branch into several fans; plant in rich soil with up to 3 inches of water over crown; full sun; overwinter as houseplant.

PARROT'S FEATHER
Myriophyllum aquaticum
6–18 inches tall
Zones 7–11
Aquatic perennial with long stems covered with small, deeply cut, lacy leaves. Small, yellowish flowers in summer. Can be invasive in warm climates; full sun; rich soil in pot submerged in 6 to 12 inches of water.

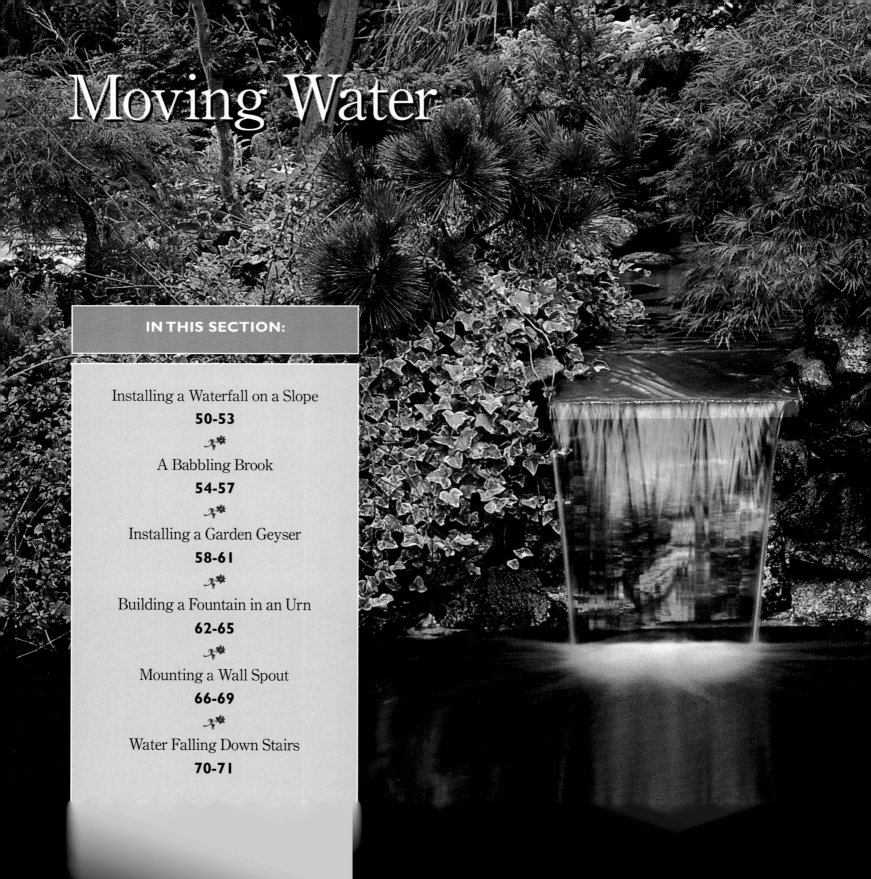

Moving Water

IN THIS SECTION:

Whether you harness a stream to move through your landscape, build a waterfall, or construct a fountain, the sound of running water adds a musical note unmatched by any other garden feature. Its fluid movement elevates a simple water feature to an enchanting oasis. Because you and your garden visitors will be drawn to the flowing water again and again, you'll want to make it easily accessible and on view from a comfortable vantage point.

The projects in this section emphasize the allure that water holds in the garden. Among them you will find one that blends into your landscape. A garden brook suits a low, narrow space in the country, while a quieter flow is more desirable through channels in formal settings. Where only the suggestion of a stream is the best solution, consider a stone-lined dry creek bed or a raked-sand Zen garden.

Several projects deal with water moving from one elevation to another. Here are fountains and waterfalls that can be incorporated into ponds of any size or, where space is limited, constructed independent of standing water. If pets and small children will have access to this garden feature, consider installing a geyser that bubbles through pebbles and rocks. An even simpler solution is a tabletop fountain or an urn for a sunroom or patio. An accompanying pump and filtration system will keep the water fresh and maintenance at a minimum. ❧

Installing a Waterfall on a Slope

Water tumbling into a pool adds sound and movement to your landscape. Waterfalls help aerate the pool and increase the filter efficiency. For best results, locate the pump away from the waterfall at the opposite end of the pond. Use stone, mortar, and a flexible pool liner to create a waterfall that drops from a small reservoir or hidden outlet into a pool.

Consider the characteristics of your existing landscape, as well as design principles, such as proportion and scale, mystery, and style, in your planning. A long, wide drop of water may create too much noise or appear out of place in a small landscape, for example. Instead, create two or three small cascades that each drop only a few inches. To add drama, curve the falls or hide the water source beneath a rock so that the entire feature is not visible all at once. As you build your waterfall, experiment with water from a hose to judge the effect. When you are satisfied, mortar the stones in place.

The height, as well as the width, of the waterfall determines the pump capacity you need. Be sure that the reservoir pond is large enough to accommodate the volume of water in the waterfall when the pump is turned off. ❧

SIMPLE WATERFALL

Compact soil with a tamper and pour concrete pads to support boulders before lining. Embed rocks in the ground to look as if they've been there for years. To keep water from running back under stones, extend the spill stone 1 to 2 inches beyond its support stone. 🌿

HAVE ON HAND:

- Carpenter's level
- 2 x 4 board
- Tape measure
- Rope
- Shovel or spade
- Fabric underlayment
- Flexible pool liner
- Glue for sealing pool liner
- Mortar
- Stones, various sizes and shapes
- Concrete trowel
- Pebbles
- Garden hose and water source
- Black plastic sheeting
- Pump and plumbing supplies, per manufacturer

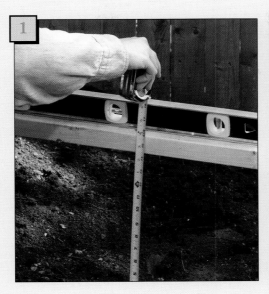

Set one end of a carpenter's level on a board at top of waterfall. Extend it over the entry point of the existing pond. Measure the vertical drop.

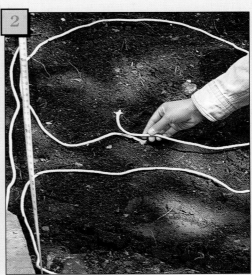

Find height between each level by dividing measurement in Step 1 by number of levels you want. Mark positions on the ground with rope.

Dig waterfall course and plumbing trench next to it. Pools must be level in all directions. Add extra depth and width for rocks. Check levels often.

Calculate liner size by measuring course from widest and longest points. Add depth and 2 feet of overlap at top, bottom, and sides.

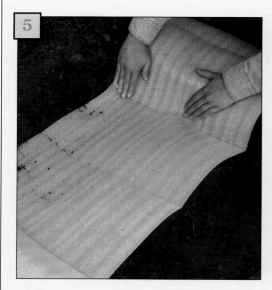

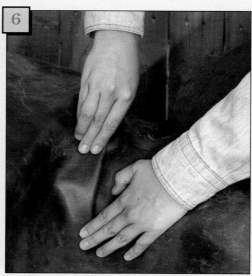

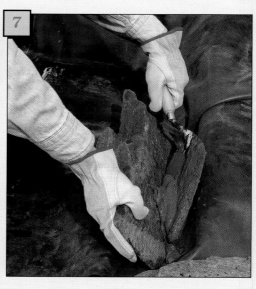

Irregular surfaces like rocks need a fabric under-layment to cushion them. Position fabric before installing liner.

Place liner in excavation, leaving overlap at sides and at pond entrance. Point folds downstream. Glue waterfall liner over pool liner. Mix mortar.

Starting at bottom, build sides first, setting stones in 2-inch bed of mortar. Use mortar behind lower stones to anchor upper stones.

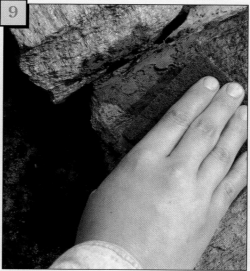

Position the spill stones and check their level carefully. Mortar remaining stones in place and hide exposed mortar with pebbles.

Wipe mortar smears off stones. Spray the waterfall lightly with water and cover with black plastic. Allow the mortar to cure for 3 to 5 days.

Run the plumbing from the pump in the pond through trench to the top of the waterfall. Adjust water flow to achieve desired effect.

Alternatives

A WIDE CASCADE

Although you will find that many waterfalls are constructed on rocky hillsides, it's possible to build one where the ground is relatively horizontal. It's best, of course, to locate a pond and watercourse where there is some contour to the land. You can increase the slope and add to the vertical drop by mounding up soil that you excavate from the pond cavity or water reservoir. Faced with a minimal change in elevation, put the emphasis on the width of the cascade rather than on its height. A wide, sheetlike flow has its own fascination and intrigue as it falls into a quiet pool.

If rocks are a component of the natural terrain or fit easily into the setting, by all means incorporate them into your waterfall; otherwise, consider facing the fall with other materials. Contemporary designs often incorporate various metallic facades or innovative concrete finishes. For original modernistic styling, consider a plastic, acrylic, or resin surface for the waterfall and the reservoir.

As you lay out your cascading water garden, carefully calculate the water volume and install a compatible submersible pump to recirculate water from the lower basin to a smaller one at the top of the fall. ❀

WATERFALL IN A BARREL

To create a garden waterfall without excavating or laying out a very complicated design, place a lined half-barrel against an existing wall where you can access an outdoor GFCI receptacle for running the submersible pump. (See page 31.)

If your stone wall is mortared or has a wood facing, you will need to drill through to run tubing behind it from the pump in the barrel to the point of the waterfall. In a dry stone or brick wall, simply loosen two sections. To complete the watercourse, run tubing from the pump, over the barrel back or side rim, through and behind the wall to a point above the barrel where water will fall. In a stone wall, allow the water to flow over a protruding stone as it falls into the barrel; in a wood or mortared fence, use a thin bamboo or copper spout.

A light, slow trickle falls musically in an intimate garden setting, but for a more pronounced sound to mask background noise, increase the rate of flow and vertical drop of the falling water. For a finishing touch, conceal the tubing in the barrel by setting potted plants in the pool. Be sure to use types such as water iris and canna that tolerate flowing water. ❀

A Babbling Brook

Streams make safe, dramatic water gardens for narrow spaces. They can empty into a pond or hidden reservoir, from which the water will circulate back to the top of the stream. Although the site must slope gently from top to bottom, the stream is divided into short sections, each of which is level from side to side and front to back. Think of a stream as a stairlike series of small pools, connected by 3- to 6-inch-high spillways. Deeper pockets behind the spillways allow water to pool and fall over the spill stones into the next section.

When you design your stream, vary its width, making the narrowest points at the spillways for increased water velocity. Use larger boulders to create diversions in the water flow. Incorporate planting pockets for marsh plants at the edges of or in the middle of the stream. Choose stone to match the style of your landscape and native surroundings and position it so that it appears natural.

Line the streambed with flexible pool liner, and cover the streambed with small stones. Mortar the spillway and other large stones in place. Place stones within the stream to deflect and divide the watercourse and increase the bubbling sound of the water.

BUILDING A SHORT STREAM

Make a natural-looking stream from flexible pool liner and cover it with stone set in mortar. A series of small pools cascade from top to bottom, emptying into a reservoir that contains a recirculating pump. To calculate the gallons of water that the pump will need to move and the size of the reservoir to accommodate it, see pages 38 and 56. ❧

HAVE ON HAND:

- Rope
- Tent stakes
- Wooden stakes
- String
- Line level
- Tape measure
- Shovel or spade
- Carpenter's level
- Boulders and stones
- Concrete mix
- Wheelbarrow
- Hoe
- Concrete trowel
- 1½-inch, reinforced, black vinyl tubing
- Flexible pool liner
- Submersible pump

Use rope to outline a U-shaped stream. Modulate width between 2 and 3 feet with curve near top to hide water source. Pin rope with tent stakes.

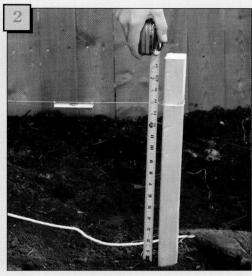

To measure vertical drop, set stakes at top and bottom of slope. Extend a string from ground level at top stake to level point at bottom stake.

Dig a shallow streambed with a series of level sections, separated by 3- to 5-inch vertical drops. Make pockets for partly buried stones.

Experiment to find best stone arrangement and location of short, level sections where water will pool before dropping to the next section.

Make concrete ledges to hold spillways between pools. Pour 4- to 6-inch-thick concrete pads to support stones weighing over 200 pounds.

Dig an 8-inch-deep, narrow trench beside stream for piping. Install 1½-inch, reinforced, flexible, black vinyl tubing in trench. Attach pump.

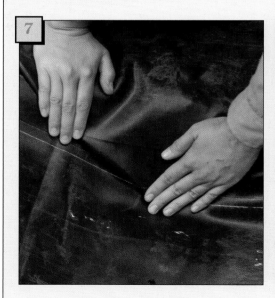

Install the liner, making folds that lie in the direction of the water flow. Overlap the stream's sides by 2 feet to avoid leaks.

Position stones in and around stream, anchoring in place with concrete. Extend liner above water level behind rocks. Hide liner under soil or gravel.

HERE'S HOW

CHOOSING PUMP CAPACITY

Capacity is measured as the gallons of water per hour a pump can lift 1 foot above the pump. To choose the correct pump size, first determine the vertical head height, which is the distance between the outlet pipe at the top of the water feature and the pump. To that measurement, add 1 foot for every 10 feet of pipe through which the water will pass. Example: 24-inch vertical head height + 12 inches for 10-foot pipe = 3-foot head.

Determine the gallons of water per hour (GPH) required to achieve the desired effect. Assume 150 GPH per inch of spillway width as standard. If the width of the spillway is 6 inches, you need a pump that delivers 900 GPH at the required head height. Consult manufacturers' charts to find the correct model.

Alternatives

JAPANESE-STYLE DRY STREAM

Traditional Japanese gardens emphasize simple form and the harmony of natural elements. Stone, wood, and water work together. In a dry garden, sand or small gravel, which is raked to resemble ripples, replaces the water.

To get this effect, construct a dry stream of sand or gravel and place groups of large stones, usually of differing sizes, at strategic viewing spots around it. Single specimen rocks may create islands in the stream. Use rounded cobblestones for beaches. Arrange the stones so that they look like a landscape in miniature as viewed from a distance.

Instead of intensively planted beds and borders, Japanese gardens depend on individual specimen plants, such as azaleas, Japanese maples, and bamboo, to serve as focal points. The plants are chosen for their architectural form, such as horizontally spreading conifers, weeping cherry, and clumping bamboo. Use color subtly. Place spring-flowering azaleas and cherries, red-leafed maples, blood grass and hakone grass carefully in the landscape.

To add the sound of water, install a buried reservoir and place an overflowing stone bowl over it. Let a bamboo pipe spill water into the bowl.

DRY WOODLAND STREAM

Create a natural-looking woodland stream without water. A dry stream makes a good alternative in settings where safety or tree roots and falling foliage make a water feature impractical. To achieve the sound and movement of water without creating an entire stream, install a hidden geyser that bubbles gently over a mossy rock.

Set stones as you would for a natural watercourse, but skip the liner. Instead, make lined planting pockets beside the stream and within it for ferns and wildflowers that prefer moist soil. Perforate the flexible liner to allow water to drain, but fill the pocket with heavy, fertile soil. Bury an irrigation pipe in the soil for easy and discreet watering. Add a weathered stump or log for a realistic effect.

Select and install plants that grow naturally beside streams in your area. Use moisture-tolerant shrubs and trees, such as shadbush or serviceberry, viburnums, spicebush, and dogwoods, to shade and enclose the stream. Plants that enjoy shady, damp soil include maidenhair, royal, and cinnamon ferns; Turk's cap lily; primrose; meadow rue; globe flower; violets; tiarella; and buttercups.

Installing a Garden Geyser

Bring cool, soothing water into your garden with a childproof geyser. A garden geyser consists of a recirculating pump hidden in an underground reservoir, which is covered with a grate and concealed with stones. A fountain, spouting sculpture, or overflowing container spills water through the stones and back into the reservoir.

You can choose from a wide variety of fountain styles to fit into any landscape. A formal fountainhead sends up a plume of water in different patterns and heights, depending on the nozzle and pump capacity. Install sculptures of fanciful animals or classically themed statues so that the water output falls over the hidden reservoir. Overflowing millstones and containers such as wooden buckets and smooth granite urns likewise match any theme.

Keep the reservoir full to accent the sound of water splashing on the stones or lower the level to add dripping sounds. Control the volume of water by installing a flow-regulator valve on the pump output. All the water should fall back into the reservoir. Soften the effect of the fountain with moisture-loving plants. Plant trailing varieties in the soil adjacent to the feature and let them creep over the wet stones.

ADDING A SPRAY

Install this easy and effective water feature in one morning. Choose a site near a GFCI-protected electrical outlet to prevent accidental damage and shock. Screen the fountain from strong winds that may blow its spray away from the reservoir. ❧

HAVE ON HAND:

- ▶ GFCI electrical receptacle
- ▶ Reservoir tub or small plastic trash can
- ▶ Shovel
- ▶ Sand
- ▶ Carpenter's level
- ▶ Trowel
- ▶ Plastic sheeting
- ▶ Scissors
- ▶ Fountain pump
- ▶ Fountainhead
- ▶ Flow valve
- ▶ Extension tube
- ▶ Wire mesh or hardware cloth
- ▶ Wire snips
- ▶ Decorative stones

Dig a hole slightly wider and deeper than reservoir tub. Add a layer of sand to bottom of hole.

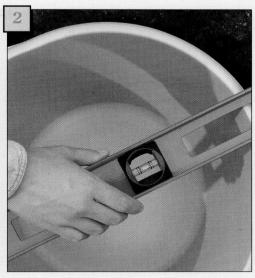

Set reservoir into hole so lip is level and flush with the ground. Use a carpenter's level to check. Backfill with sand, and adjust as needed.

Slope the soil around the tub slightly toward hole so water will run into tub when soil is covered with plastic.

Cut plastic sheeting large enough to catch and direct water from fountain into tub. Fit over tub; cut hole 2 to 4 inches smaller than tub opening.

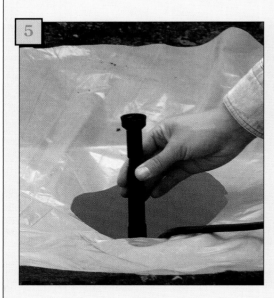

Connect the pump to the fountain, flow valve, and extension tube. Place in tub and adjust to the desired height.

Fill the tub with water to within a few inches of the top. Test the pump and fountain, and adjust the flow rate, if needed.

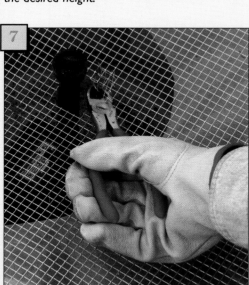

Cut a circle of wire mesh 18 to 24 inches wider in diameter than tub. Cut a small hole in center to accommodate fountain tube.

Cover the wire mesh and plastic sheet with stones in a decorative or natural pattern.

HERE'S HOW

FOUNTAINHEAD STYLES

Fountainheads offer a wide array of spray patterns depending on the size, number, and placement of holes in the nozzle. Some send up a single plume or jet of water, while others can give a two- or three-tiered effect. Mushroom fountains make a bell-shaped dome of water. Bubblers send up a low, frothy gush. Some fountains even whirl around, driven by the water pressure from the pump. Individual spray jets attached to a pipe can be positioned to shoot water in any direction. Choose a fountainhead to match the style of your water feature and landscape.

Clean fountainheads occasionally with a mineral-dissolving solvent, such as white vinegar, to prevent nozzles from clogging. Use opaque black tubing to keep algae from growing in and blocking the lines.

Alternatives

PLANTS FOR A GARDEN GEYSER

Choose plants that enjoy moist soil but do not require submerged roots, and that can tolerate some water splashing on their leaves. Consider the style of the geyser when selecting plants. If the fountain itself is a decorative statue, for example, use plants that blend into the background and subtly accent the water feature. Surround simple geysers, however, with more colorful flowering and foliage plants.

Place the garden plants outside the perimeter of the reservoir and space them so that they will not crowd the fountain or interfere with the water spray as they mature. Place tall, bold plants behind the fountain to act as a background or foil for the water. Use creeping and low-growing plants to mask the transition from the decorative stones to the surrounding garden soil.

Near shady garden geysers, plant hosta, astilbe, ferns, and primrose. For sunnier sites, try sedges, grasses, and the flowering plants described below. Keep the soil moist around the geyser. Divide and replant pieces of the more vigorous plants when they outgrow their space.

SIBERIAN IRIS
Iris sibirica **'Crème Chantilly'**
30–36 inches tall
Zones 3–8
Narrow, grasslike leaves form dense clumps; flowers in late spring to early summer in colors ranging from white to deep violet; thrives in moist, fertile soil but is also drought resistant; full sun to light shade; remove spent flowers after blooming.

LIGULARIA
Ligularia dentata **'Othello'**
30–36 inches tall
Zones 4–8
Clump-forming perennial with large, round-toothed, purplish green leaves beneath yellow flowers borne on dark-stemmed spikes up to 3 feet high in summer; sheltered spot with moist, fertile soil; part shade to full sun with noon shade.

BEE BALM
Monarda **'Mahogany'**
30–36 inches tall
Zones 4–9
Vigorous, clump-forming perennial with light green leaves and rounded clusters of red, tubular flowers in summer. Foliage is richly aromatic with fragrance like bergamot; rich, moist soil; full sun; location with good air circulation helps control powdery mildew.

ASTILBE
Astilbe x *arendsii*
30–36 inches tall
Zones 4–8
Glossy, dark green leaves divided into toothed leaflets may have reddish tinge; plumes or spikes of white, pink, red, or purple flowers in summer; plant in moist, fertile, slightly acidic soil in part shade; divide every four years to maintain vigorous growth.

WHORLED LOOSESTRIFE
Lysimachia punctata **'Alexander'**
24–36 inches tall
Zones 4–8
Vigorous but noninvasive perennial with medium green leaves and strong stalks sporting whorls of bright yellow flowers in summer; moist but not sodden soil near pond or stream edges; full sun to part shade; divide every four years.

Building a Fountain in an Urn

Simple and elegant, a bubbling fountain brings soothing sound and movement to an outside patio or indoor room. Here, a small urn is supported on a bed of water plants at the top of a large stone. Water pumped through hidden tubing attached to a recirculating pump in the catch basin beneath the stone flows from the tipped urn and cascades over the stone back to the basin.

Choose an urn or other container that matches the style of your home and is deep enough to completely submerge the pump and wide enough to contain the fountain spray. The fountain can trickle water gently over the stones or send up a small jet of water into the air, depending on the desired effect and pump capacity. If the water splashes out of the urn, adjust the flow with a control valve.

You can add plants to the urn for color and softness. Plant parrot's feather, dwarf sweet flag, and creeping Jennie in discarded nylon stockings filled with aquatic plant potting soil and tuck them under the stones. Provide full sun for the plants year-round to keep them healthy and replace or divide them as they outgrow the container. Add water to the urn as needed to keep the water level above the pump intake at all times.

SPILLING WATER

Construct a simple tabletop or patio-sized water feature from an urn. Add a recirculating pump, fountain nozzle, and decorative stones to suit your décor and provide the appealing sound of bubbling water. Plants, grown in fabric mesh bags, turn a fountain into a miniature water garden. 🌿

HAVE ON HAND:

- One or more flat stones
- Unglazed ceramic urn
- Polyurethane spray
- Tape measure
- Fountain pump
- Flexible black tubing
- Foam sealant
- GFCI outlet
- Restrictor clamp or valve (optional)
- Terra-cotta planter
- Pantyhose
- Aquatic plant potting mix
- Trowel
- Water hyacinth, creeping sedum, and ivy
- Goldfish (optional)

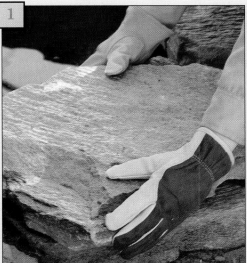

Use flat stones or one large stone to make a sturdy platform for the urn in the center of the pond.

Apply polyurethane spray to unglazed ceramic urn. Be sure to coat inside of pot evenly. Let dry for 24 hours, and then apply second coat.

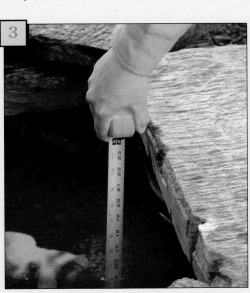

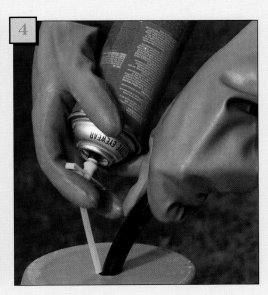

Measure the lift (distance from floor of pond to platform) to determine correct pump to use. Set pump in pond.

Attach flexible hose to pump. Thread hose through drainage hole of urn. Seal hole around tube with foam sealant.

Plug the water pump into a GFCI outlet and test the fountain. Adjust the flow, if needed, with a restrictor clamp or valve.

If space allows, accent the urn with a shallow terra-cotta planter. Fill planter with water and add floating plants, such as water hyacinth.

Make additional planters by pouring aquatic plant potting mix into sections of pantyhose; tie ends. Lay planters around urn to stabilize it.

Make slits in pantyhose and fill planters with low-growing plants, such as creeping sedum and ivy. Release goldfish into pond.

HERE'S HOW

POND AERATION

Increasing the amount of oxygen in your pond water helps prevent the buildup of toxic gases, such as carbon dioxide and sulfur dioxide, and dissolved toxins, such as nitrites and ammonia. Aeration becomes especially important in hot weather and in ponds containing fish.

Disturbing the pond surface increases the aeration or amount of oxygen in the water. Waterfalls and fountains are the most common and effective aerators. For the best water circulation, place the pump inlet and outlet at opposite ends of the pond. Use a fountain with a vigorous spray for maximum aeration.

Alternatives

A TABLETOP FOUNTAIN

A small fountain brings the lulling sound of moving water indoors or to a garden tabletop. Unlike a more complicated outdoor version, a fountain in a basin takes little effort to establish. You may already have a favorite ceramic or metal container that you'd like to display. To transform this into a fountain, check to see that its reservoir is deep enough to hold a small pump and enough gravel or rocks to conceal it. Here's a place for favorite collected stones, polished rocks, or even seashells. Arrange them so they balance a small pot set on top at an angle. The pot can be an existing flowerpot with a predrilled drainage hole or a pot with a solid bottom that can be drilled.

Use a grindstone bit to perforate a solid ceramic pot, working slowly and patiently so as not to break the clay. It helps to keep the drill area cool if you pour a slow, steady stream of water into it as you drill. Enlarge the hole to ⅜ inch wide and fit flexible tubing from the pump through the bottom hole. Set the pump flow control at medium or lower and fill the basin. With the pump running, assess the impact of the moving water. Adjust the flow and rearrange the pot as needed to prevent spills and splashes. 🍃

A BAMBOO SPOUT

Garden pools and fountains need not be elaborate to be impressive. The sound of gurgling water in a small pool not only beckons to the garden visitor but offers up-close viewing. You can transform a sculpted bowl, ceramic pot, or metal tub into an exciting miniature water feature and give it a place of honor alongside a deck or patio or wherever there's a nearby electric outlet. It is also less complicated to install than a larger pond and requires less maintenance. Wood and ceramic containers may require a plastic lining or sealant to prevent seepage.

If the container you choose is too small to hold a submersible recirculating pump, set the pump underneath or alongside in a buried catch basin. Cover the basin with hardware cloth and camouflage the entire assembly with stones. Run tubing from the pump to the fountain through the bottom of the container and seal the opening securely with cork, cement, silicon, or other appropriate sealant.

A very small water feature is easiest to manage when it is completely independent of plants. Use it as a garden accent in a quiet shaded spot or move it into a sunny site with flowering potted annuals. 🍃

Mounting a Wall Spout

Wall-mounted fountains fit into even the smallest spaces, either indoors or out in the garden. Among the simplest water features to construct, wall masks are also among the most dramatic. Usually, a sculptural face adorns the spouting side, while the flat back mounts against a wall.

A complete wall spout fountain consists of the mask, a catch basin, and a pump with tubing to recirculate the water. Some wall fountains include the mask and basin as one piece, and these are the simplest to install—simply hang securely, add water, and plug in. Always be sure to plug water pumps into a GFCI-protected receptacle.

Other wall spouts consist of separate components. Purchase or make your own flat-backed mask and drill a hole in it for the waterspout. Make the hole the same diameter as the plastic tubing that connects to the pump output. Choose a basin to complement the mask or position it above an existing pool and place the water pump within it. Attach the mask to the wall permanently with mortar or hang it temporarily from hooks or screws. If possible, install the plumbing and electrical service out of sight behind the wall. ❧

WALL MASK WITH BASIN

Add drama and the sound of running water to even a postage-stamp-sized patio with a simple wall fountain. Use one that's already drilled for plumbing or make your own from an attractive statue or mask. Choose a catch basin wide enough to contain the splashing water. Marsh and aquatic plants, such as parrot's feather, creeping Jennie, and papyrus, soften the edges and help prevent excessive algae growth. ❧

HAVE ON HAND:

- Half-barrel (to waterproof, see page 13)
- Tape measure
- Wall mask
- Mounting screws
- Screwdriver
- Flexible black tubing
- Fountain pump
- Electric drill and bit slightly larger than diameter of tubing
- GFCI outlet
- Leafy and cascading plants
- Garden hose and water source
- Electrical outlet
- Flow regulator (optional)

Use a half-barrel or other basin that doesn't require special installation. Position and level the basin on ground at base of wall.

Check specifications to determine how high pump can lift water. Measure maximum lift from water surface; mark on wall.

Use screws to secure wall mask to wall so spout is below mark for maximum lift.

Attach flexible black tubing to the fountain pump. Put the pump in the bottom of the basin. Fill basin with water.

Drill hole slightly larger than diameter of tubing from back of wall to wall spout. Drill another hole through wall near lip of basin.

Run tubing from pump through hole near lip behind wall, then back through the wall to the spout on the back of mask.

Plug pump into a GFCI outlet. Disguise any cable or tubing with leafy plants, such as ferns, or cascading plants, such as ivy.

Use flow control on pump to adjust water flow for desired look and sound.

HERE'S HOW

CHOOSING TUBING

Flexible tubing and rigid PVC pipes come in a range of sizes starting at ½ inch. The pump capacity and length of the run determine which size you need. Long distance and large pump capacities require larger diameter tubing. Use adapters, if necessary, between differing tube sizes.

The diameter of the pump outlet is usually appropriate for the tubing size, but if the pipe length exceeds 50 feet, consider increasing the diameter by ½ to 1 inch. In general, ½-inch-diameter tubing is adequate for up to 120-GPH pumps, ¾ inch for up to 350 GPH, 1 inch for up to 1,000 GPH, 1½ inches for up to 3,000 GPH.

Alternatives

SPOUTING FOUNTAIN

Animals and other classical statues make intriguing fountains for both casual and formal gardens. Use them as focal points or place them in the landscape where visitors will come upon them unexpectedly. Combine elements to create unique water features. Position a spouting fish so that it sprays water into a small pool, for example, or put a bubbling frog on a log or stone over a hidden reservoir.

Hide the plumbing within the feature for the best appearance. For a statue in a birdbath, run the tubing through a concealed hole in the birdbath and seal it with silicone sealant. As an alternative, use water plants to cover the tubing. Classical Greek and other statues often appear in formal, round stone basins that overflow into hidden reservoirs. Place the statue on a pedestal that has been drilled to conceal the tubing and position the submersible pump in the bottom of the reservoir or basin.

Choose a pump that can move a stream of water to the necessary height and volume. Pumps are rated by their gallons-per-hour output at 1 foot above the pump. The diameter of the tubing also affects discharge capacity. Install a flow-control regulator and adjust it as desired.

TILTING BAMBOO FLUTE

A shishi-odoshi, or "stag scare," is a traditional Japanese fountain made of bamboo. A bamboo spout drips water into a rocking bamboo tube below it, which fills with water and when full, tips, spilling its load into a pool or hidden reservoir. As the tube empties and returns to its upright position, it strikes a stone and makes a sound that reportedly frightens deer.

The spout and rocking tube are held between two upright bamboo pieces, which can be pushed into the soil to hold them in place. The rocking tube swings on a dowel between the uprights. The dowel must be positioned so that the bottom of the rocking tube rests on the stone behind the fountain when empty, but easily tips forward when filled.

Attach the spout to one of the bamboo uprights after drilling holes in both pieces so that a small water tube can pass through. Connect the tube to the pump, which is located in the pool. Adjust the water flow so that it fills the rocking tube without splashing. For best effect, place this water feature in a quiet location away from strong winds, which will disrupt the water flow.

Water Falling Down Stairs

Use the natural slope of a stairway to create a series of cascading waterfalls. Let the sound of flowing water greet visitors or install the feature on your deck steps for a soothing background melody. Build this project as a seasonal waterfall or allow it to run year-round in mild climates or even indoors.

Use shallow containers to hold and spill the water smoothly from one step to the next. Make your own from copper, waterproofed wood, or ceramic, or look for suitable ready-made containers at kitchen or garden supply stores.

The pump that operates the waterfall sits in a catch basin hidden beneath stones at the base of the bottom step. Choose a pump size that will create a smooth, vigorous cascade of water from one step to the next. In the uppermost container, hide the water source under a stone or overhanging plant foliage.

Calculate the necessary pump size as described on page 56. Choosing an inadequate pump size will result in the water's trickling down the front of the containers instead of flowing smoothly. The reservoir must be large enough to keep the pump submerged while supplying adequate water. Add water as needed to keep the pump covered. 🌼

CREATING A SPILLWAY

In water-conscious climates, water features can seem extravagant, but several strategies keep them water-efficient. The most important step is to eliminate all leaks through the liner and around the edges. Keep waterfalls and fountains low. Use a timer to turn them off when no one is around to enjoy them, unless they are part of a biological filtration system needed for fish health.

If this waterfall is in a windy location, protect it with a wind-screening fence or hedge. ❧

HAVE ON HAND:

- ▶ Containers for waterfalls (of equal size with smooth, narrow, straight spillways)
- ▶ Shovel
- ▶ Plastic tub for reservoir
- ▶ Modeling clay
- ▶ Submersible pump
- ▶ Flexible black tubing
- ▶ ½-inch wire mesh, to cover reservoir
- ▶ Smooth stones or pebbles
- ▶ Water source
- ▶ GFCI electrical receptacle

Set containers on each stair, overhanging edge slightly. Excavate for reservoir at base of bottom stair; leave a 1-inch rim above ground.

Tip containers slightly so water is deepest at spilling edge. Experiment with flowing water to find best angle. Prop with modeling clay.

Set pump into reservoir. Fasten a length of flexible black tubing to output. Extend it to back of top container, concealing it behind stairs.

Cover reservoir with wire mesh and conceal with smooth stones. Fill reservoir; plug pump into ground fault circuit protected receptacle.

Planting around Water Gardens

Plants are an integral part of water gardens, if not submerged in pots, then adorning the periphery. Naturalistic designs most commonly use plants both in the water and out to smooth the transition from water to the surrounding landscape, often blurring the water's edge. More formal watercourses usually feature only a limited number of plants growing directly in the water and focus instead on the artistry of the water's flow.

In the projects that follow, you'll find plants of all types, from trees to grasses, linking water features of various styles to their surroundings. A few projects, such as the Japanese garden and the lotus in an urn, invite contemplation and relaxation more than gardening, while most others call for more active participation. For ponds in woodland settings, wildflowers are an ideal planting. Gardeners in warm climates will be interested in the project featuring tropical plants—many of which can be overwintered in more northerly zones. Where ponds freeze in winter, water gardens call for special attention, and plants with year-round interest are an added benefit.

Throughout this section are ideas for companion plantings that create ambiance. But you'll also find ideas for construction and plumbing. One of these projects or an alternative to it will help you find the water garden just right for your landscape. 🌺

A Natural Woodland Water Garden

Create a woodland pool that seems to bubble up from a hidden spring. If you already have a shady spot near a tree or at the edge of the woods, add this small water feature to highlight it. Take care not to disturb too many tree roots when excavating the pool, however, and avoid placement near trees that drop lots of leaves or those that cast dense shade.

After installing the lined pool, blend it into the landscape with stones, lush planting, and shredded leaves or natural bark for mulch. Add a small recirculating pump and direct its output to trickle gently over a mossy rock. A fallen log can serve as a seat from which to enjoy the shaded pool. If space is limited, build a hidden geyser instead of a pool, using a stone placed over a buried reservoir.

Around the pool, plant woodland ferns, wildflowers, and woodland shrubs native to your area. Use a few plants with silver, gold, or white variegated foliage to brighten the shade and accent the darker greens and colorful flowers of other plants. Add a touch of the exotic with potted tropical plants that you can move around and use to fill in between the hardier, permanent plantings. ❧

PLANTING A WOODLAND POOL

Woodland pools, often only a few feet across and no more than 12 inches deep, provide water and habitat for many birds and small animals. Use a flexible pool liner, small submersible pump, and natural stones, mulch, plants, and wood to create a shady sanctuary. Make a wide planting bed around the water feature; add shade and moisture-loving plants to blend the transition from water to the larger landscape. 🌿

HAVE ON HAND:

- ▶ Spade or shovel
- ▶ Carpenter's level
- ▶ Fabric under-layment
- ▶ Flexible pool liner
- ▶ Water source and hose
- ▶ Rocks
- ▶ Mulch

Plants
- ▶ Summersweet or witch hazel
- ▶ Variegated hosta
- ▶ Japanese painted fern
- ▶ Arrowhead
- ▶ Dwarf tropical water lily
- ▶ Variegated sweet flag

Excavate a hole 12 to 15 inches deep with vertical sides. Adjust shape and size to suit surroundings. Berm edge slightly, and be sure it's level.

Install soft fabric underlayment and a flexible liner. Overlap the sides by about 12 inches. Fill with water to settle the liner.

Set rocks for a trickling spring along edge of pool on extended section of liner. Hide water source within a naturally arranged pile.

Plant one summersweet or witch hazel 5 feet from the pool. The shrub will grow into an attractive screen and backdrop for other plants.

5

Plant a large-leafed white or gold-variegated hosta 4 to 5 feet from summersweet at edge of pool. Add fern clumps to mask pool edge.

6

Plant arrowhead and a dwarf tropical water lily in pots. Place pots in the pool.

7

Plant variegated sweet flag between the other perennials to brighten the shade.

8

Cover the exposed liner and soil around the pool with natural mulch, such as shredded leaves, pine needles, or bark. Keep soil moist.

HERE'S HOW

TRIMMING AND MOWING

Keep grass clippings out of your pool by planning ahead for lawn maintenance. For ponds edged with stone, bricks, or wood, make a wide mulched planting bed between the edging and the lawn. If your mower throws the clippings, be sure to mow so that grass flies away from the water garden.

For lawn-edged ponds, use a bagging mower that collects the clippings. Trim the very edge of the pond with a string trimmer before mowing, so that the mower will pick up the debris. Remove clippings from the pond with a pool net as soon as possible to prevent their decaying in the water.

Alternatives

FOCUS ON FERNS AND WILDFLOWERS

Ferns and wild-flowers make the perfect companions for woodland pools. Many fern species, such as lady fern, shield fern, ostrich fern, sensitive fern, Japanese painted fern, and Christmas fern, thrive in damp shade and moist but well-drained, humus-rich soil. Given these ideal conditions, they'll spread and grow into large, feathery colonies.

Spring wildflowers brighten shade under the forest canopy. Foamflower sends up spikes of starry white flowers in early spring, and the maple-leaf-shaped foliage makes an attractive ground cover. Smooth phlox, with pale pink to violet flowers, blooms at the same time. Other spring-blooming wildflowers for a shady pool include spring beauty, violets, and bleeding heart. For summer, add Turk's-cap, Canada, or wood lilies, as well as anemone, bee balm, and mallow.

Use shrubs as background plants and to add privacy. Those that grow naturally in light shade include mountain laurel, fothergilla, camellia, rhododendron, daphne, and many viburnums. Choose shrubs with colorful blooms or berries, such as winterberry, chokeberry, and shadbush, to attract birds and extend the ornamental display.

A SHADY SEAT

Pull up a chair and relax in the shade by your soothing woodland pool. The weathered wood of a comfortable armchair blends with the stone edge of the goldfish pool. The mossy stones form a natural basin at the edge of the forest. A pump and filter clean the water and provide a gentle trickle over a mossy rock, which imitates a natural spring.

Plants blend the pool with the surrounding forest edge. Hostas—some with bold, white-edged leaves and others in chartreuse or gray-green—brighten the shade and contrast with creeping ground covers, such as creeping Jennie, sweet woodruff, and mint. The low-growing plants fill the gaps between stones and soften the hard edge. Many also cover themselves with a carpet of flowers in spring or summer.

Add color with potted annual flowering and foliage plants. Impatiens bloom in shades of pink, red, and white all summer long. Some have double, roselike flowers. Other popular flowering annuals for shade include browallia, begonia, and forget-me-not. For colorful annual foliage, pot up red leaf caladium or coleus, which grow in a rainbow of hues, shapes, and sizes.

A Formal Reflecting Pool

Formal water gardens focus on pool architecture rather than plants. Most formal pools have geometric shapes, such as circles, ovals, squares, and rectangles. Well-defined, hard edges made of bricks or paving stone add to the formal appearance. Display fountains or simple weir waterfalls may help circulate and aerate the water, depending on the desired effect, planting design, and presence of fish.

The still water of a reflecting pool mirrors the surrounding landscape, making small spaces seem larger and connecting disparate or imposing spaces. Large, formal water features look best with formal, architecturally designed buildings and landscapes. Small pools, however, can work effectively even in small, informal settings.

In natural and informal ponds, plants grow close together, hiding the edge. The architectural edges of formal water features usually remain exposed. Specimen plants, such as water lilies, lotus, and papyrus, often accent the garden, but do not compete with the overall design or hide the edges of the pool. Formal pools that are at least 3 to 4 feet deep may also house koi.

BUILDING A FORMAL POOL

Build an oval formal pool and line it with flexible pool liner, as described on page 33. Make straight vertical side-walls without plant shelves. Slope the bottom slightly toward a sump hole or low spot for easier draining. Hide the liner behind a course of bricks or pavers set into the wall at water level. Cover them with square or rectangular paving stones set around the edge in concrete, as described on page 41. 🌸

HAVE ON HAND:

- ▶ Tape measure
- ▶ Wooden stakes
- ▶ String
- ▶ Spade
- ▶ Fabric under-layment
- ▶ Flexible pool liner
- ▶ Water source and hose
- ▶ Mortar
- ▶ Wheelbarrow and hoe, to mix mortar
- ▶ Pavers
- ▶ Mason's trowel
- ▶ Sponge

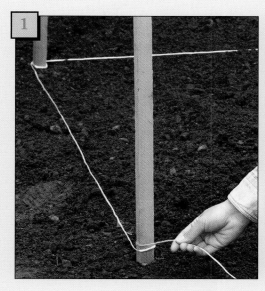

Measure desired pool area and place wooden stakes at corners. Tie string to base of stakes to outline perimeter of pool.

Use square-edged spade to excavate pool. Bottom of pool should be flat and sides clean and straight.

Use a spade to excavate shelf for pavers. Shelf should be depth of pavers, which will be placed around the perimeter in Step 6.

Place fabric underlayment in base of pool and along sides. Underlayment should cover shelf and extend about 6 inches beyond.

Install pool liner over underlayment. Fold corners and gently press into position. Fill pool about halfway to settle liner.

Mix mortar in wheelbarrow. Spread a 1-inch layer of mortar along shelf on top of liner. Set pavers in place along shelf, spaced ½ inch apart.

Fill gaps between pavers with mortar and smooth with the tip of mason's trowel. Check frequently to be sure pavers are level.

Allow mortar to set for a few hours, then wipe with wet sponge to remove excess. Let mortar cure for 48 hours before completely filling pool.

HERE'S HOW

KOI FACTS

Over the past 200 years, Japanese koi enthusiasts have developed more than 100 different varieties of koi, known as *Nishikigoi* in Japanese. These colorful carp grow up to 3 feet long and can live for decades. Koi require well-aerated and filtered water that is at least 3 to 4 feet deep. Each mature fish needs 25 to 50 square feet of surface area. Koi dig and tend to uproot and eat plants while foraging for food.

Koi range in price from a few dollars to many thousands of dollars, depending on the shape, color, pattern, size, and rarity of the fish. They can be trained to do tricks and often become favorite pets. Join a hobbyist group or attend a koi show to learn more.

Alternatives

PLANTS FOR A REFLECTING POOL

Plants used in formal pools, such as lotus and water lilies, often play a starring role in the overall design. Water lilies root in soil on the bottom of the pool or grow in pots. Their round leaves float on the surface and may be green or mottled with red. Water lilies are categorized as either tropical or hardy. Tropicals need year-round water temperatures between 50° and 70°F. Hardy water lilies survive freezing winters as long as the water in their container does not freeze.

Tropical water lilies bloom during either day or night, and their flowers range from white to yellow, pink to blue-purple, and red. Hardy varieties flower in white, pink, red, and yellow. Some hardy water lilies remain dwarf in size, making them more suitable for growing in tubs and small pools.

Lotuses grow and flower best where water temperatures remain 75° to 85°F. They hold their huge, waxy, round leaves above the water, and their rose, yellow, or cream blooms fade to reveal decorative seed pods. The large plants need plenty of space to spread—containers at least 3 feet in diameter are ideal. You can grow dwarf or bowl lotus in smaller quarters. ✿

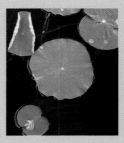

SACRED LOTUS
Nelumbo nucifera
2–6 feet above water
Zones 4–11
Round leaves up to 30 inches across on stems as tall as 6 feet; flowers resemble peonies and form when water temperatures remain 75° to 80°F; grow in rich soil in large pots submerged in 15 to 24 inches of water; full sun; protect from freezing.

HARDY WATER LILY
Nymphaea
Floating
Zones 4–11
Round, notched leaves 4 to 12 inches across float on surface, spreading up to 6 feet; flowers open in morning and close in afternoon; grow with 12 to 20 inches of water above the crown; avoid splashing water on leaves.

TROPICAL WATER LILY
Nymphaea
Floating
Zones 10–11
Leaves up to 14 inches across, some with crinkled edges or purple streaks, spreading up to 12 feet; flowers are held above the water and open either day or night; overwinter as described on page 25.

LADY'S MANTLE
Alchemilla mollis
18–24 inches tall
Zones 3–7
Mounding perennial with round, medium green, wavy-edged, toothed leaves. Small, greenish yellow flowers appear in late spring to early summer. Moist, fertile soil (but it's also drought tolerant); part sun. Deadhead flowers after bloom.

GRAY SEDGE
Carex pseudocyperus
6 feet tall
Zones 7–11
Marsh plant with pointed, oval, gray-green leaves on long stalks; violet flowers on tall stems above the leaves; forms dense clumps in rich, fertile soil; allow up to 12 inches of water to cover the crown and fertilize monthly.

Making a Welcoming Entrance

Take advantage of a natural slope at the front of your house or transform a difficult-to-mow hillside into a natural-looking pool and waterfall that masks the sound of passing traffic and welcomes visitors. Use water, stones, and plants on a slope to create a dramatic focal point or, on more level ground, add a subtle stream that meanders from a hidden reservoir to a quiet pool near the front door. For a more natural look, excavate so that at least one-quarter of each large stone is below ground.

The entrance to your home must be safe and welcoming. Avoid water features such as fountains, geysers, and vigorous waterfalls that could spray water across the walkway, wetting visitors and making the path slippery. Make paths adjacent to streams and ponds from slip-resistant gravel or roughened concrete and keep them free of algae and moss.

Shrubs, trees, and perennials blend the pool into the landscape. Tuck plants into pockets of soil between boulders. Plant small trees or large shrubs, such as Japanese maple, rhododendron, or dogwood, to soften the edges and add color. Let a few plants arch or weep over the edge to hide portions of the water garden and create a sense of mystery. 🌸

ENTRYWAY WATER GARDEN

C reate a hollow space behind the waterfall to increase the volume of sound that the water produces. Calculate the needed pump capacity as described on page 56. Divide the flow by placing stones at the edge of the falls, or encourage the water to spill over in a smooth sheet by directing the water over a level spill stone. Allow water to pool behind the waterfall to add force to the flow. ❦

HAVE ON HAND:

- Shovel or spade
- Pry bar
- Carpenter's level
- Stones of various sizes
- Mortar mix
- Fabric underlayment
- Flexible pool liner
- Water source and garden hose
- Submersible pump
- Tubing
- Potting mix

Plants

- Shrubs, trees, and perennial plants
- Marsh plants in pots

Excavate a slope to create 2 levels separated by a vertical drop for the waterfall. Dig an adjacent trench in which to bury tubing from the pump.

Dig pools at top and bottom of waterfall. Be sure perimeters are level from side to side.

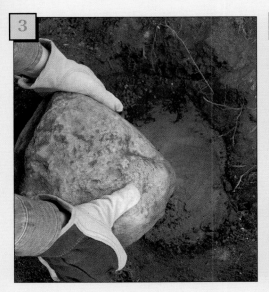

Design and test placement of large boulders. Use a pry bar to maneuver heavy stones. Set stones aside until needed in Step 6.

For boulders weighing more than 200 pounds, dig 6 to 8 inches deeper; pour concrete support pads. Allow concrete to set.

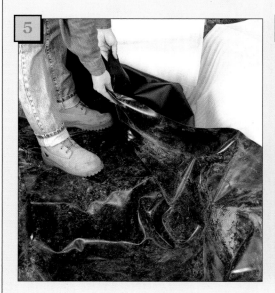

Line entire excavation, including waterfall, with underlayment and a flexible pool liner. Overlap the sides by at least 2 feet to prevent leaks.

Arrange boulders and small rocks as planned in Step 3. Fill upper reservoir to test water flow. Adjust spill stone. Anchor stones with mortar.

Allow mortar to cure. Fill pool with water and install pump and tubing. In the top pool, hide the water source under a stone.

Plant shrubs and small trees near pool and waterfall. Fill gaps between rocks with soil; add perennials. Place potted marsh plants at edges.

HERE'S HOW
WATER DEPTH PLANNER

Your climate and the types of fish and plants you include in your water garden determine the appropriate depth of your pond. You can create shelves and pockets at various depths to accommodate plants with differing needs, or use underwater supports, such as bricks or overturned crates.

Here are the guidelines for planning water depths:

- **Koi:** 3 to 5 feet
- **Goldfish:** 2 to 3 feet
- **Large water lilies:** 2 feet
- **Dwarf water lilies:** 12 to 18 inches
- **Marsh plants and lotus:** 2 to 12 inches, allowing up to 6 inches of water above the soil

Alternatives

SOUTHWEST STYLE

Doors that face the southern sun heat up in the summertime, parching plants and making the entryway uncomfortably hot. Cool the area off with a narrow pool fed by a wall-mounted waterfall. Add plants that tolerate drought for a low-maintenance, welcoming entry.

When you build the water feature, raise it 18 to 24 inches above the entrance patio and make the edge wide enough for seating or holding packages. Hide the plumbing behind the wall in a closet or utility room.

To add Southwest flair to the pool, use red adobe tiles with colorful accents of cool turquoise, bottle green, black, and creamy white. Set a row of tiles on the diagonal and outline the row with narrow tiles in a darker color. Use the same tile, colors, or patterns in the patio floor to create a cohesive look.

Add a planting bed at the base of the pool and fill it with plants that can take the heat and arid conditions of the site. Choose gray-leafed wormwood, rosettes of hens and chicks, and succulent kalanchoe and sedums. Other good flowering plants for dry gardens include Mexican primrose, dwarf oleander, Spanish lavender, and South African daisy. 🌼

ACCENT PLANTS FOR AN ENTRANCE

Turn a level courtyard entrance into a lively oasis of colorful flowering annuals and dramatic foliage plants. Some long-blooming, easy-to-care-for, cheerful pansies brighten a dark entrance and also enliven neutral paving stones and concrete. Other popular annuals for planting around a raised water garden include petunias, zinnias, impatiens, and nasturtiums. Repeat the colors or plants in adjacent flower beds to unify the garden.

Plants with white-striped foliage, such as variegated Japanese sedge, sweet flag, and umbrella sedge, add contrast. For a strong vertical element, try giant horsetail, papyrus, bulrush, or cattail. If your garden is large, add a plant with very bold foliage, such as Chinese rhubarb or a Siebold hosta. You can cover the water surface with soft-textured parrot's feather, creeping water poppy, or yellow fringe flower.

A geyser adds the soothing sound of moving water. Adjust the water flow to keep the spray low enough to prevent splashing onto the sidewalk. As an alternative, place a spouting fountain on the edge of the pool. Potted plants and sculptures break up the strong geometric lines of a raised water garden, softening the edges. 🌼

An Evening Garden Pool

A garden pool is an enchanting oasis anytime, but it becomes even more enticing after dusk. Tucked into a hidden nook or in full view beneath an open sky, a garden pool is irresistible under moonlight. Pale flowers and foliage floating on the surface or planted around pool margins emerge as dim beacons. Evening air and exotic blossoms set the stage for many enjoyable evenings outdoors. As a bonus, many white flowers release their most intense fragrance in the evening and attract various moths that feed on their nectar.

For interest over several seasons, intersperse blooming annuals and perennials with grasses and shrubs around your garden pool. Among all of the white-flowering plants, night-blooming tropical water lilies are some of the most beloved and highly scented. Consider a mock orange shrub and peonies for spring; Asiatic lilies, daisies, and phlox for summer blooms; and asters and mums for fall. In a small space, plant in pots that you can change with the seasons. Add plenty of pale foliage. Catmint, baby's-breath, lavender, and lamb's ears are just a few plants that impart a luminous, silvery quality in evening light. ❦

WATER GARDEN BY NIGHT

Awater garden that is designed to be enjoyed in the evening as well as during daylight hours can bring in a touch of romance and mystery, along with peace and tranquillity. Plants that stand out in moonlight include those with gray or silvery leaves as well as those with white or pale-colored flowers. Be sure to leave the southern horizon open to maximize the amount of moonlight entering the garden. 🌿

HAVE ON HAND:

- ▶ In-ground pool with flexible liner
- ▶ Large stones
- ▶ Statue or other garden ornament
- ▶ Marble chips

Plants

- ▶ White or light pink water lilies
- ▶ Ornamental grass
- ▶ Caladium or lamb's ears
- ▶ White or pale pink perennials

Install a garden pool with a flexible liner in an open area with a southern exposure. Make pool at least 2 feet deep to accommodate water lilies.

Set a pot of white- or light pink-flowered water lilies in deep section of pool.

Group clusters of large stones near edge of pool. Set each stone in a shallow pit a quarter the height of the stone.

For a focal point, install a light-colored, small statue or other garden ornament on the stones, a few feet from the edge of the pool.

Set a few clumps of plants with gray or variegated leaves, such as caladium or lamb's ears, near the pool.

Plant clusters of ornamental grasses like maiden grass as background for garden ornament and flower beds.

Plant groups of white- or pink-flowered perennials, such as sedums, garden phlox, lilies, or rose mallow, around the pool and garden.

Brighten paths near the garden by covering the walkway with a layer of marble chips. Use marble chips as a mulch around ornamental grasses.

HERE'S HOW

ENHANCING REFLECTION

Gazing globes have long been used to introduce color and interest in gardens. Alongside a garden pool, their shiny surface and classic beauty mimic reflections on the water surface, adding another dimension to an evening garden. The traditional globe is made of clear, silvered glass, but you can now find them in all colors, polished stainless steel, and copper.

Place your gazing globe on a carved pedestal in an open area for a focal point, or set it on a plain post nestled among plants near the pool. Or, try floating one in the water.

You can also enhance reflection in the evening garden by dangling sparkling glass whimsies from tree and shrub branches or by hanging a mirror on a wall or fence. Any evening reflection is emphasized when you place low-voltage uplighting at ground level to highlight your favorite plants.

Alternatives

PLANTS FOR AN EVENING GARDEN

Plant your garden with white or pale-colored flowers and foliage that gleam in the twilight. Line garden paths with white annual petunias or silvery artemisia, and add taller plants as accents throughout the garden. Use them to draw your eye through the night garden by placing them at curves in a path or by clustering them by a bench or other destination. White-flowering water plants are especially effective against the dark pond surface.

Fragrant flowers are often more intensely perfumed at night. White-flowered Oriental lilies, tall varieties of nicotiana, sweet William, and sweet alyssum combine intense fragrance and evening glow. Plant chamomile or creeping thyme between path stones where they will release their scent as you walk on them. Consider white and fragrant-flowered shrubs, such as summersweet, daphne, gardenia, and many viburnums.

Sound is amplified in the evening, making splashing and dripping water, peeping frogs, and the rustle of leaves and grasses more noticeable. Tall rushes, cattails, and ornamental grasses, especially those that have silvery or white-variegated leaves, add ambiance to your night garden. ❧

JAPANESE IRIS
Iris ensata
24–40 inches tall
Zones 4–9
Green, swordlike leaves; large, single, or double, white to red-purple flowers in early to midsummer; grow in very moist soil with the crowns just above water; full sun; choose white flowers for best evening viewing.

NIGHT-BLOOMING TROPICAL WATER LILY
Nymphaea
Floating
Zones 10–11
Round, notched leaves float on surface, spreading up to 10 feet; white-flowering varieties, such as 'Trudy Slocum', 'Sir Galahad', and 'Juno' open at dusk and close late morning; plant in large baskets and fertilize monthly.

VIRGINIA SWEET SPIRE
Itea virginica **'Henry's Garnet'**
5–10 feet tall
Zones 6–9
Upright deciduous shrub with medium green leaves and long, slightly drooping spikes of mildly fragrant, cream-colored flowers in summer. Foliage turns bright red in fall; full sun to part shade; moist, rich soil at edges of streams or ponds.

VARIEGATED SWEET FLAG
Acorus calamus **'Variegatus'**
24–36 inches tall
Zones 4–11
Striped green and creamy white, swordlike leaves resemble large grass blades; provide a wide pot to give creeping rhizome room to grow; place in shallow water with 1 to 6 inches of water over the crown; fertilize monthly in summer; full sun.

WHITE CALLA LILY
Zantedeschia aethiopica
15–36 inches tall
Zones 9–11
Arrowhead-shaped leaves on long stalks; elegant chalicelike white flowers throughout the summer; grow in rich soil with up to 2 inches of water over the crown; fertilize monthly; overwinter in nonfreezing place in damp soil.

Creating a Tropical Oasis

Whether you live in a real tropical climate or just want to imitate one, creating a water garden oasis will add lush elegance to your landscape. In naturally cool climates, aboveground pools located in full sun will warm up more quickly in the spring and give you a longer season of tropical flowers and foliage than in-ground pools. Gardeners in hot summer climates, on the other hand, can partially shade their pools with palms and other trees that hold their foliage year-round. Installing the pool in the ground will stabilize the water temperature and help prevent overheating.

To give your water garden a tropical appearance, use bold-textured plants lavishly. Garden centers and many home improvement stores sell palms, rubber trees, taro, and other tropicals as houseplants, which easily adapt to outdoor living for the summer. Use these around the perimeter of the pool. Add colorful canna, calla, and water lilies for tropical bloom. Include terra-cotta, wood, bamboo, or stone accents, such as a tile patio or wood pergola for vines.

The tropics host many mosses and ferns. Build a grotto waterfall of porous stone and surround it with natives of the rain forest, such as orchids, bromeliads, and scrambling vines.

TROPICAL POOL

Combine several basic water garden building and planting projects to make a haven of tropical sights and sounds. Add a fountain urn to an above-ground pool. Set tubs of water lilies and marsh plants in and around the pool, and cover the sides with creeping vines, blending the pool into the landscape. 🌺

HAVE ON HAND:

- 24-inch-deep aboveground pool
- Terra-cotta urn
- Spouting fountain kit
- 2 sealed cement blocks
- Shovel
- Potting mix
- Trowel
- Goldfish (optional)

Plants
- Banana or palm tree (about 4 feet tall)
- Agapanthus
- Water lilies
- Upright marginal plants, such as cattail or arrowhead
- Ground cover in 4-inch pots, such as ivy
- Floating and submerged plants

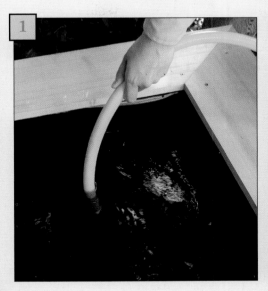

Construct a formal, 24-inch deep, aboveground pool and line it with flexible pool liner. Cover top edge with a wide board for seating.

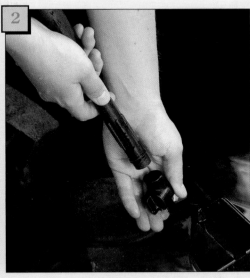

Make an overflowing fountain from a terra-cotta urn. Pump water from pool through a spout in the urn. Support it on sealed cement blocks.

Plant banana or palm, either in a pot or in the ground, where it can cast midday shade on the pool or nearby seating.

Near the fountain, plant an agapanthus or another dramatic plant with attractive foliage that flowers for many weeks.

Add 2 water lilies to pool, choosing varieties that grow well in your climate and that bloom at the time of day that you are likely to view them.

Plant pots of low-growing marsh and marginal water plants and set them on cement blocks inside the perimeter of the pool.

Plant vines, such as ivy, in the ground around 2 or 3 sides of the pool. Train the ivy to cover the pool sides as it grows.

Add goldfish, if desired, as well as floating and submerged plants to control algae.

HERE'S HOW

OVERWINTERING PLANTS

Keep tropical plants through the winter by taking them indoors as the nights get cooler, but before frost threatens. Most tropicals need high humidity and bright light for at least 14 hours a day to remain healthy. Mist daily with a spray bottle or place them on trays of wet pebbles, but don't let them sit in water unless they are water plants. Supplement natural daylight with fluorescent lights.

In late spring, begin reacclimatizing plants to outdoor living by gradually exposing them to sun and wind. Initially move them outside only on cloudy, calm days. For the first few weeks, avoid strong sunlight and wind, which could scorch or tatter the leaves.

Alternatives

PLANTS FOR TROPICAL LANDSCAPES

Bold foliage and bright flowers characterize a tropical pool, which includes trees, shrubs, perennials, and annuals that grow around the pool as well as in it. Gardeners in tropical climates have many plants from which to choose. Those living in more temperate climates can achieve a tropical effect by growing a mix of exotic-looking hardy plants and tropicals that spend the winter indoors.

Hardy plants that look tropical include staghorn sumac with its palm-frondlike leaves and spikes of red flowers, large-flowered clematis vines, and dramatic ornamental grasses. Annual plants and flowers, such as amaranth and castor bean, add boldly colored foliage. You can also grow some tropical plants as annuals, disposing of them at season's end. Other tropical plants, such as palms, can go indoors as winter houseguests.

Store canna, caladium, dahlia, begonia, and other tender tubers and bulbs in a cool, nonfreezing place.

Most tropical water plants must be overwintered indoors or replaced annually in freezing climates. A few, such as papyrus, make attractive houseplants if kept in a saucer of water in a sunny window.

WATER HYACINTH
Eichhornia crassipes
4–6 inches tall
Zones 10–11
Floating tender perennial with glossy, round leaves, lavender-purple roots, and a spike of pale purple flowers in summer. Full sun; grows best when water temperatures are above 60°F; classified as noxious weed in several warm climate states.

UMBRELLA PLANT
Cyperus alternifolius
18–36 inches tall
Zones 10–11
Whorls of straplike leaves atop tall, green stems; spiky, greenish brown flowers; some varieties remain shorter, and 'Variegatus' has white-striped leaves; grows with up to 6 inches of water above the crown; overwinter as a houseplant; full sun to part shade.

ANGEL'S TRUMPET
Brugmansia spp.
6–15 feet tall
Zone 11
Fast-growing shrub with very large, fragrant, trumpet-shaped flowers that hang from woody stems; white, yellow, pink or reddish blossoms; well-drained, moist soil, full sun; excellent container plant. Keep away from children and pets, as all parts are toxic if ingested.

CANNA
Canna 'Pretoria'
4–6 feet tall
Zones 8–11
Large, green leaves with prominent, closely spaced, yellow stripes; large, yellow, apricot, red, or orange flowers in summer; grow in moist soil at water's edge or adapt to 2 to 6 inches of water over the crown; fertile soil and full sun.

THREE-WAY SEDGE
Dulichium arundinaceum
1–3 feet tall
Zones 3–9
Slender stems covered with thin, green leaves resembling bamboo. Can form thick mats in sodden ground or shallows. Helps attract wildlife to water gardens; full sun.

Establishing a Meadow Pond

A still-water meadow pond suggests wide-open spaces, but you can custom build one in nearly any backyard. By surrounding your pond with sun-loving ornamental grasses, patches of wildflowers, and drifts of low-maintenance perennials, you can transport the natural, informal atmosphere of an open meadow to your water garden. Seasonal flowers, fruits, and seeds throughout several seasons are sure to bring birds, butterflies, and other wildlife to the water's edge. For harmony and contrast, choose long-blooming species such as ox eye daisies and black-eyed Susans, sages and mallows, purple coneflower and goldenrod, achillea and monarda. Soften pond edges by planting low, arching species along a shallow shoreline.

Meadow ponds often have rounded shapes and uneven margins, though farm ponds are often rectangular. A clay bottom provides an ideal liner for any shape in a natural setting, but either a rigid or flexible pool liner is preferred for small backyard ponds. Though size is dependent on the site, give your pond a depth adequate for maintaining a healthy ecological balance. Keep in mind that a deep area of cool water is essential if you plan to add fish. ❧

SUNNY PRAIRIE POND

A s you plant around the perimeter or inside the pond, consider the root structure of nearby plants. Avoid siting your pond too near very large trees with shallow roots, which can interfere with or even penetrate the lining. To prevent rampant growers such as cattails and horsetails from taking over a small pond, corral their colonies in containers. You may need to run a water line for your plants or for refilling a small pond. Large meadow ponds depend on rainfall and runoff to maintain their water level. ❧

HAVE ON HAND:

- ▶ Spray paint
- ▶ Shovel
- ▶ Flexible pool liner
- ▶ Water source and hose
- ▶ Fish
- ▶ Frogs or tadpoles

Plants

- ▶ Deep-water plants
- ▶ Emergent plants
- ▶ Wetland plants
- ▶ Prairie wild-flower seeds
- ▶ Shrubs to feed and shelter birds
- ▶ Water-loving shade trees

Mark perimeter of pond with spray paint, and excavate. Install flexible pool liner. Grade shore-line. Fill pond with water.

In small ponds, grow deep-water plants, such as lotus and water lilies, in pots. In large ponds, plant directly in pond bottom.

In shallow water and wet spots along the shore, use emergent plants, such as cattails, arrowhead, and yellow flag iris.

In moist areas near shore, plant wetland types, such as Joe-Pye weed, boneset, cardinal flower, and water iris.

Sow prairie wildflowers, such as black-eyed Susan, perennial sunflower, gayfeather, and coreopsis, in well-drained banks above pond.

To provide shelter and food for birds, plant clusters of shrubs, such as red osier or gray dogwood and holly, around the shore.

To shade the pond and keep the water cool, place water-loving shade trees, such as river birch, hemlock, or white pine, along the shore.

Introduce fish and frogs into the pond to help control mosquitoes and other pests.

HERE'S HOW

LINING WITH BENTOMAT

Bentomat is a type of pond liner made from woven material and fine granules of bentonite clay. Although it is fairly expensive, this specialized liner is well suited for large natural ponds because it forms a secure, watertight bottom. Its fibrous surface is impervious to tree roots and burrowing animals on the outside; on the inside, it is covered with a 12-inch layer of topsoil where noninvasive marginal water plants may be grown. Work loose bentonite granules into the subsoil under the natural pond to provide additional waterproofing.

Alternatives

PLANTS FOR A PRAIRIE WATER GARDEN

Prairie plants withstand sweeping winds and often harsh winter conditions. The fertile prairie soil, however, supports a rich tapestry of grasses, shrubs, and annual and perennial wildflowers. Purple coneflower, daisies, gayfeather, and columbine attract butterflies and color the landscape. Native grasses bend and rustle in the wind.

Choose native, moisture-loving plants to surround the pond. Create pockets of moist soil by burying a perforated pool liner and filling it with fertile soil. Water regularly. Plant aggressively spreading aquatic and marsh species, such as cattails and horsetails, in pots or large containers and set them at the edge of the pond, or place them so that up to 6 inches of water covers their soil.

Instead of exotic water lilies and tropical plants, grow native spatterdock, bullhead lily, pickerel weed, and arrowhead. Edge the pond with low-growing grasses, rushes, reeds, and cattails instead of stones. Add a partially submerged log to attract birds, turtles, and frogs. Or build a low island within the pond and plant it with marsh-dwelling wildflowers or a shrub. ✻

JOE-PYE WEED
Eupatorium spp.
4–6 feet tall
Zones 3–9
Tall, strong stalks with whorls of large, lance-shaped leaves and flat-topped clusters of purple-pink flowers in late summer and fall. Prefers full sun and rich, moist to wet soil along pond edges. Blossoms attract late season butterflies. Vigorous grower that can become invasive.

CATTAIL
Typha latifolia
4–6 feet tall
Zones 3–11
Long, straplike, dark green leaves rise from crown in fan shape. Strong, central stalk bearing brown, fuzzy flower in summer. Full sun; sodden soil or shallows; divide every 3 years.

NARROW-LEAF CATTAIL
Typha angustifolia
60 inches tall
Zones 2–11
Long, narrow, straplike leaves rustle in the breeze; brown flower and seed heads on tall stalks in summer, persisting through winter; plant in moist to wet fertile soil; confine its spread in pots or enclosed planting bed.

ARROWHEAD
Sagittaria spp.
12–36 inches tall
Zones 5–11
Marginal perennial with dark green, arrowhead-shaped leaves rising a foot or more above the water. Spikes of white flowers bloom in summer to fall. Full sun; grow in rich soil with 6 inches of water over crown.

YELLOW FLAG
Iris pseudacorus
3–5 feet tall
Zones 5–8
Very large, vigorous perennial forming clumps of swordlike foliage. Bright yellow flowers appear above leaves in late spring and early summer. Full sun; sodden soil at water's edge or shallows.

Lotus in an Urn

The sacred lotus, cherished for centuries in Asia, offers dedicated water gardeners elegant flowers and foliage for formal pools and large containers. Among the more difficult water plants to grow well, lotus is worth the effort for its blooms. The waxy round leaves, which may reach 20 to 30 inches across, stand high above the water on stems up to 6 feet tall. Not all lotuses reach such proportions, however. Many varieties stay more compact, making them useful for container cultivation. Lotus varieties suitable for growing in a large urn or half-barrel include 'Momo Botan', 'Chawan Basu', 'Baby Doll', 'Charles Thomas', and 'Ben Gibson'.

Lotuses have fragile, easily damaged roots that need plenty of room to spread. Full-size lotuses need pots 3 feet in diameter, but dwarf varieties can grow in a container the size of a half-barrel. Newly introduced teacup or bowl lotuses, which grow only a foot tall, will grow in 12-inch-diameter pots. All require fertile soil and twice monthly fertilization. Bloom occurs after 8 to 10 weeks of temperatures between 75° and 85°F. In cold climates, protect the tuberous root from freezing by storing it in a container of moist sand at a temperature of 50° to 55°F. ❧

PLANTING A LOTUS

Handle lotus roots carefully to avoid breaking the fragile tuber and growing tips. Plant only in smooth round containers. Lotuses need only a few inches of water covering their soil surface. Feed established plants every 3 to 4 weeks in summer with aquatic plant fertilizer tablets. Place in full sun to light shade. As leaves grow and develop, gradually increase the water depth to 6 inches over the soil.

HAVE ON HAND:

- Aquatic plant fertilizer tablets
- Waterproof pot, 20 inches in diameter or larger
- Aquatic plant potting mix
- Soil
- ½-inch pea gravel

- Urn or tub, large enough to hold the 20-inch pot
- Bricks
- Water source
- Bucket

Plants

- 1 dwarf lotus 'Momo Botan'

Place 1 or 2 plant fertilizer tablets in the bottom of a waterproof, 20-inch diameter pot.

Fill the pot with potting mix made for water plants to within 2 to 3 inches of the top.

Lay the lotus root on the soil surface with the cut end against the side of the pot.

Gently add ½ to 1 inch of soil, keeping the soil away from any growing shoots.

Put a thin layer of gravel or stone over the soil surface, again taking care to keep it away from any growing shoots.

In the bottom of the urn, put bricks on which to place the potted lotus so that no more than 2 inches of water will cover the lotus root.

Fill the urn with warm water (75° to 80°F). Avoid cold water, which can shock the lotus and delay growth.

Set potted lotus gently into water, disturbing soil as little as possible. As leaves grow, add more water, up to 6 inches above the soil.

HERE'S HOW

OVERWINTERING FISH

Fish living in shallow ponds and small water gardens may need indoor housing for the winter in cold climates. Goldfish, kept in aquariums or wading pools for the winter, need cool (70°F or lower), filtered water and at least 2 gallons of water per inch of fish. In other words, one 5-inch goldfish needs a 10-gallon aquarium.

Prepare the aquarium by mixing about one-third pond water with dechlorinated tap water. Set up the filter and aeration. If possible, float the captured fish in an inflated plastic bag in the aquarium for 20 minutes to equalize the water temperatures. Siphon and replace one-fourth of the water each week to remove waste. Once a day, feed only what the fish can eat in 1 to 2 minutes.

Alternatives

TROPICAL WATER LILIES

Aristocrats of the garden pool, tropical water lilies hold their flowers slightly above the water on stiff stems. The star or cup-shaped blooms open in shades of white, yellow, pink, red, purple, and blue, depending on the variety. So-called day-blooming lilies open in midmorning and close in the afternoon. Night-blooming lilies open in the afternoon and close the next morning, making them a good choice for people who enjoy their garden in the evening and early morning. Many tropical lilies have fragrant flowers—great for pools where you can get close to the blooms.

Tropical water lilies cannot tolerate freezing temperatures and grow poorly in cool water. In cold winter climates, you can store the fleshy rhizome in clean, distilled water in a cool place. Remove all leaves, roots, and clinging soil before storage. Replant in spring in the pond, in full sun, when the water warms to 70°F. Or, grow them through the winter in a heated greenhouse.

The floating round to oval leaves may be green or splotched with purple, smooth edged, wavy, or serrated. The largest plants can spread to 10 feet, while smaller varieties grow to half that size. ❦

HARDY WATER LILIES

Hardy water lilies are easier to grow than their exotic looks would suggest. Most will grow in any pond in which water remains unfrozen under the ice, though some are not reliably hardy in areas where temperatures fall below 0°F. Most have flowers that open in midmorning and close by late afternoon, but some, such as the petite yellow 'Helvola', stay open into the evening. Flower colors include yellow, white, peach, pink, and red.

Plant spread ranges up to 6 feet across, but small varieties, including 'Helvola', apricot 'Chrysantha', white 'Hermine', deep pink 'Froebelii', and 'Perry's Dwarf Red', stay about half that size, making them good candidates for patio tubs. Flowers open and close for 3 days before sinking below the surface. Remove spent flowers and leaves regularly to keep them from decaying in the pond.

Pot up the rhizomes with the growing tips just above the soil and place aquatic plant fertilizer tablets in the bottom of the pot to encourage lush growth and plenty of flowers. In the fall, place the pots in the deepest part of the pond where the water will not freeze, or lift and store as described for tropical water lilies. ❦

Landscaping Ponds for Winter Interest

In cold climates, the winter pond becomes a flat sheet of ice, but thoughtful planting keeps the surrounding landscape interesting, even in the bleakest of seasons. Evergreens and trees with architectural branching habits contribute their unique forms to the winter landscape. Ornamental grasses with persistent seed heads or stiffly upright stems rustle softly in winter breezes and add a vertical element to the pond landscape. Cattails, reeds, and rushes give similar effects at the pond's edge.

Shrubs with colorful bark, such as red osier dogwood and green-stemmed Japanese kerria, add color. Trees and shrubs with autumn and winter bloom, such as witch hazel and heath, give a burst of color when it's most appreciated. Seek out plants with early spring bloom and underplant them with spring-flowering bulbs.

Ornamental objects serve as important focal points in all seasons, including winter. A stone statue, gazing ball, or sundial draws attention to the pond, while bird feeders, placed well away from the water's edge, bring delightful activity to a backyard pool. Use a pond heater to keep a bit of open water near a handy perch to provide the birds with a much-needed drink. ❧

A PLAN FOR WINTER

Choose a vantage point from which to view your pond in winter. Place ornamental statues, bird feeders, and plants with winter features where you can see them readily. When choosing plants for winter interest, look for colorful or textural bark, unusual branching habit, and persistent foliage or berries. Place bird feeders and trees that drop foliage and berries away from the pond to prevent leaves, berries, and other debris from falling into the water. 🌺

HAVE ON HAND:

- ▶ Landscape fabric
- ▶ Edging stones
- ▶ River stones
- ▶ Sculpture or ornamental boulders
- ▶ Birch or hemlock trees
- ▶ Dwarf spruce or Japanese pines
- ▶ Swamp holly
- ▶ Rhododendron, heavenly bamboo, or mahonia
- ▶ Ornamental grass

Remove vegetation at far end of pond from natural vantage point. Cover soil with weedproof landscape fabric and fasten with pin.

Hold landscape fabric in place with large stones set at pond's edge.

Spread river stones over area around larger stones to create a "beach." If desired, position sculpture or large boulders as focal points.

Plant birch or hemlock trees 25 to 35 feet behind the pond and at the sides to provide background interest.

5

Plant 3 to 5 dwarf conifers, such as spruce or Japanese pines, across from the large ornamental stones on the beach to echo their arrangement.

6

Plant shrubs with attractive fruits, such as swamp holly, a few feet from the edge of the pond.

7

At the sides and near end of pond, plant flowering evergreen shrubs, such as rhododendron, heavenly bamboo, or mahonia.

8

Grow clumps of ornamental grass, such as miscanthus, in a sunny location near the water.

HERE'S HOW

WATER GARDEN IN WINTER

Water gardens in cold winter climates need special care in the autumn as temperatures drop toward freezing. Ponds containing hardy fish need air exchange year-round to prevent the buildup of toxic gases. To keep a small area of open water, add a floating pond heater or float a large ball in the water. In milder climates where temperatures remain below freezing for only a few days at a time, a plastic tent over the water can prevent ice from forming.

Disconnect and drain all plumbing. Place potted hardy water plants in the deepest part of the pool to protect them from freezing. Take tender plants indoors for the winter. Cover pool with a net to keep leaves and other debris out of the water.

Alternatives

ORNAMENTAL STATUES AND STONES

When snow covers the ground and green plants and flowers are just a memory, other ornamental features become the focus. Although deep snow may hide all but the largest or tallest features, infrequent or light snow leaves edging, stones, and statues visible above a frozen pond's surface.

Choose stone or wood to outline your pond. Vertical rounded wood edging accents a section of shoreline and highlights a tree, shrub, or statue placed behind it. Stone edging provides a dark contrast to the glistening snow. Large stones placed near the pond, either individually or as groups, also add drama and interest. Shadows and the play of light and dark draw the eye toward a grotto or cairn of stone. Dry waterfalls, streambeds, and rocky shores become dramatic with dripping ice and snow.

Statues are particularly intriguing in winter. Japanese lanterns stand sentinel at the pool by day and can provide candlelight for evening walks in the early winter dusk. Spouting statues, drained of water, remain ornamental in all seasons. Choose statues made from weather-resistant materials, such as bronze and concrete, if you plan to leave them outdoors through the seasons. ❧

TREES AND SHRUBS

Trees and shrubs give your garden structure and a sense of permanence year-round. Some water gardeners avoid placing trees and shrubs near ponds to avoid falling leaves and damaging roots. But not all woody plants cause extra work, and many that could are worth it.

Trees with weeping or drooping branches are particularly effective near a water garden, where they echo the movement of falling water. Look for Japanese maple, birch, cherry, katsura tree, spruce, pine, larch, and others, with varieties called 'Pendula' or with 'weeping' as part of their name. If you plant them close to the pond's edge, consider installing a transparent net over the water in fall to catch the leaves.

Brightly colored berries and fruits that remain on the plants through the winter provide food for wildlife and add color to the wintry pondscape. Winterberry, red chokeberry, firethorn, rugosa roses, and staghorn sumac offer splashes of red against the snow. Many flowering crab apples have persistent fruit, too, in many sizes and colors from deep red to bright yellow. Also look for trees and shrubs with decorative bark, such as stewartia, birch, paperbark maple, and Japanese tree lilac. ❧

Contemplating a Japanese Garden

Japanese gardens interpret in miniature a world of lakes, rivers, mountains, and meadows. Garden designers use stone, sand, earth, water, and plants to symbolically represent each element. A boulder becomes a mountain, raked sand imitates the waves of the sea, a sculpted bonsai portrays a centuries-old tree. Gardens serve as places of quiet meditation and contemplation.

Water is an essential element in Asian garden design. Gently moving water, such as a bamboo flute dripping water into a stone basin or a pool of clear water with a lotus or water lily, promotes the flow of positive energy in the garden. Water also balances the hard, immutable element of stone—another key ingredient in Japanese gardens.

The shape, color, texture, and placement of stone in the garden has strong spiritual and symbolic importance. Rocks form the bones of the landscape and, therefore, assume a central role in Asian garden design. Visual balance is key when placing stones. A large or dark-colored boulder may balance three smaller or lighter-colored stones placed nearby, for example. Designers often choose individual stones with shapes that represent magical or mythical beasts, such as tigers and dragons. ❀

JAPANESE WATER GARDEN

Stone and water, or the representation of water, are central design elements in Japanese gardens. Raking sand into waves and ripples becomes a form of daily meditation for many gardeners. Frequent maintenance keeps leaves, twigs, and footprints from marring the pristine setting. Placing the garden within a walled yard helps prevent cats and other animals from spoiling the effect. Use a narrow rake, such as a child-sized tool or one specially designed, to create the intricate patterns.

HAVE ON HAND:

- ▶ Stones of various sizes and shapes
- ▶ Edging stones or pavers
- ▶ Rope or garden hose
- ▶ Spade or sod cutter
- ▶ Turkey grit (available at feed stores) or crushed granite
- ▶ Small rake for patterning sand

Choose a level area in your yard, preferably a place surrounded by evergreen trees.

Choose stones for the garden. Use odd-numbered groupings or a large stone balanced by smaller stones. Vary sizes and shapes.

Arrange the stones, experimenting until you find an appealing placement.

Outline the area of the garden with a rope or garden hose, letting the placement of the stones and surrounding landscape suggest its shape.

Strip the sod from the garden with a spade, or use a rented sod cutter for large areas. Remove all vegetation thoroughly to prevent weeds.

Edge garden with flat stones or other unobtrusive materials that will hold sand in place and prevent creeping grass and weeds from entering.

Spread an even layer of coarse sand, such as turkey grit or crushed granite, over the area to a depth of 2 to 3 inches.

Place rocks. Rake sand around the stones into ripples that seem to emanate from the rocks. Use the stones' shape to suggest the pattern.

HERE'S HOW
FENG SHUI PRIMER

Feng shui, which literally means wind and water, is an ancient Chinese technique of placing objects and arranging the home, business, and garden environments for health, happiness, and abundant fortune. Practitioners use the points of the compass and the five elements of water, fire, earth, metal, and wood to manage universal energy, called ch'i. Ch'i flows in the same way that water and wind flow—correct placement of objects keeps ch'i moving smoothly without stagnation or rapidity. A gently curving path between colorful flowering plants, for example, promotes better energy flow than a straight path between tall, dark evergreens. Balancing opposites, such as light and dark, wet and dry, hard and soft, is also fundamental to feng shui.

Alternatives

A ZEN SPIRAL

A swirling line of smooth river stone set amid a tranquil pond exerts a soothing and inspirational effect through a subtle blend of shapes and textures. To the reflective mind, patterns laid out with plants and rock deepen the appeal of a water garden as they serve as focal points for contemplation, much like a meditative mandala or the raked sand that ripples around solid stones in a Japanese garden. Located in a sheltered site or in an out-of-the-way corner, the water garden becomes even more peaceful.

When selecting materials for a contemplative water garden, keep the notions of balance and harmony at the forefront. Choose stones of nearly equal size that are large enough to rest in place and be visible above the water level, yet will fit the overall scale of the water feature. Look over your final plan to be sure that the pool assumes a harmonious proportion with the garden as a whole.

Plants may or may not be introduced into a quiet pool. If they are, choose them on the basis of form. A simple spike such as water iris, a hardy sweet flag along the perimeter, or floating clumps of frogbit may be all you need. ❦

PLANTS FOR A JAPANESE GARDEN

Unlike lush, densely planted European gardens, Japanese gardens use plants as accents and complements to the stone and water. Moss often covers the ground and grows on rocks and boulders placed strategically in the garden. Its fine texture allows it to represent miniature grassy meadows and mountain forests viewed from a great distance. Other plants commonly found in Japanese gardens include ferns and bamboo.

Camellias and azaleas, traditional woodland flowering shrubs, become focal points in the landscape. Pines, spruce, and fir protect the garden. Junipers and other evergreen shrubs are sometimes pruned into shapes that suggest exposure to mountain winds; other times they're trained as ground covers.

Japanese maples play an important role in Oriental gardens. Their smooth, gray bark is attractive in all seasons. Many varieties exist, some with reddish or chartreuse foliage, others with unique branching habits. Maples with filigreed leaves have a very fine texture, ideal for small gardens and close viewing. Those with weeping habits resemble falling water, an important garden element. ❦

Wildlife Gardens

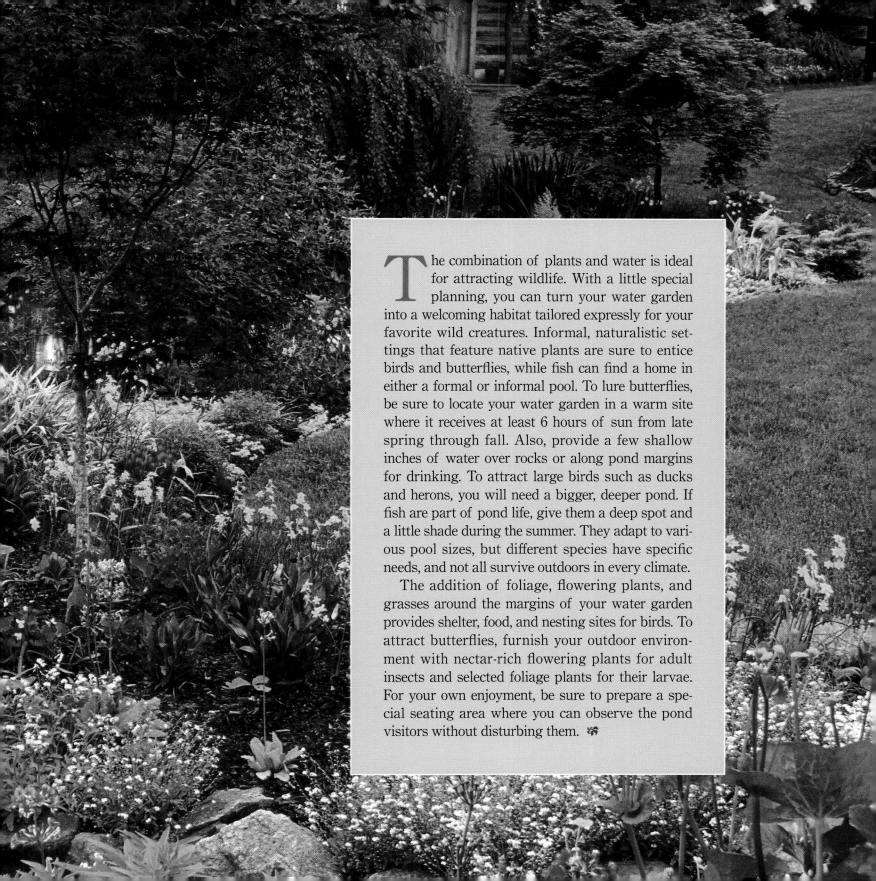

The combination of plants and water is ideal for attracting wildlife. With a little special planning, you can turn your water garden into a welcoming habitat tailored expressly for your favorite wild creatures. Informal, naturalistic settings that feature native plants are sure to entice birds and butterflies, while fish can find a home in either a formal or informal pool. To lure butterflies, be sure to locate your water garden in a warm site where it receives at least 6 hours of sun from late spring through fall. Also, provide a few shallow inches of water over rocks or along pond margins for drinking. To attract large birds such as ducks and herons, you will need a bigger, deeper pond. If fish are part of pond life, give them a deep spot and a little shade during the summer. They adapt to various pool sizes, but different species have specific needs, and not all survive outdoors in every climate.

The addition of foliage, flowering plants, and grasses around the margins of your water garden provides shelter, food, and nesting sites for birds. To attract butterflies, furnish your outdoor environment with nectar-rich flowering plants for adult insects and selected foliage plants for their larvae. For your own enjoyment, be sure to prepare a special seating area where you can observe the pond visitors without disturbing them. ❧

Attracting Butterflies

Butterflies gliding from flower to flower bring jeweled color to the garden. They come seeking food, shelter, and moisture. Plant your garden with nectar-rich plants that bloom in succession from spring to fall and provide shallow water at the edge of a pond to entice butterflies to stay. Butterflies also enjoy sun-warmed stones in cool weather.

The most butterfly-attractive gardens offer a variety of habitats, such as trees, shrubs, and flowering plants both in groves and in the open. Some species prefer wooded areas, while others flock to meadows or marshes. It's also important to provide food for the caterpillars, also called larvae, which become butterflies. Luckily, the larvae of many popular butterflies feed on common garden plants and weeds. Consult a field guide to find the preferred diet of the species you wish to attract.

Butterflies enjoy water, but they must have places where they can alight and sip in safety. Provide a shallow beach covered with sand or stones and a muddy spot to please the greatest number. In a very small water feature, such as a birdbath or trough, set a stone or piece of tree limb in the water so that part of it projects above the surface.

BUTTERFLY WATER GARDEN

Use a simple, ready-made birdbath to create a water feature that draws colorful butterflies to your garden. To entice adult butterflies, surround the structure with an assortment of plants, such as coreopsis, zinnias, and sedum. And be sure to include herbs such as dill and parsley for caterpillars to feed on. ❧

HAVE ON HAND:

- ▶ 3 large, flat stones
- ▶ Birdbath
- ▶ Carpenter's level
- ▶ Clean, white sand
- ▶ Trowel
- ▶ Small, rounded stones
- ▶ Watering can and water
- ▶ Shovel
- ▶ Annuals, perennials, shrubs, and herbs

Near the center of the garden, place flat stones to form a base for the butterflies' birdbath.

Position a ready-made birdbath on the stones. Use a carpenter's level to ensure that it is even all around.

Fill the birdbath to just below the rim with clean, white sand. Smooth with your hand or with a coarse brush.

Arrange small, rounded stones in a decorative pattern on the sand. Gently add water until sand is moist but not drenched.

5

Plant groups of hardy perennials, such as sedum, butterfly weed, and coreopsis, in the sunny area around the birdbath.

6

Grow annuals and tender perennials, such as geranium, lantana, or zinnia, in the remaining open areas.

7

Plant flowering shrubs, such as double-file viburnum and butterfly bush, in a sheltered, sunny spot near the birdbath.

8

Near the shrubs, plant dill, parsley, and other plants that butterfly caterpillers use for food.

HERE'S HOW

ENCOURAGING AMPHIBIANS

Frogs, toads, newts, and salamanders may appreciate your water garden as much as you do. These insect-eating animals lay their eggs in or near the water, and the hatchlings live their early lives submerged. To encourage adults into your pond, make a shallow beach or set logs or stones at the edge to allow them to crawl in and out of the water easily.

Water animals appreciate places to hide from predators such as herons, hawks, and raccoons. Overhanging stones and densely planted marsh plants give adequate shelter. Bullfrogs and visiting turtles will eat small fish, however, so don't encourage these creatures if your pond is home to young goldfish or koi.

Alternatives

PLANTS FOR ATTRACTING BUTTERFLIES

Adult butterflies and moths seek flowers for nectar, but their caterpillars also depend on plants for food. Most butterfly caterpillars need very specific plants for their food source. The larvae of the monarch butterfly, striped in black, yellow, and white, for example, feed only on milkweed, which later provides nectar for the adults' autumn migration. To attract butterflies successfully, grow plants that provide food and habitat for all stages of the insects. Choose a wide variety of plants that bloom throughout your growing season so that there is always something flowering.

In arid climates and soils, grow moisture-loving butterfly plants in a lined marsh garden. Pierce the pond liner so water can drain, but install a buried drip hose to provide moisture when needed. Let plants that prefer well-drained soil grow outside the lined garden, or plant them in containers.

TURTLEHEAD
Chelone **spp.**
24–36 inches tall
Zones 3–9
Easy-to-grow perennial with strong stems lined with pairs of lance-shaped, dark green leaves. Small spikes of white to pink flowers resembling the heads of turtles appear in late summer. Wet to waterlogged soil; full sun to shade.

GAYFEATHER
Liatris spicata
24–48 inches tall
Zones 4–9
Spikes of pink to purple flowers emerge from a rosette of narrow, green leaves; fuzzy flowers along the spikes open from top to bottom over several weeks in late summer.

ELECAMPAGNE
Inula helenium
3–6 feet tall
Zones 5–8
Vigorous, clump-forming perennial with rosettes of very long, green leaves. Large, daisy-like flowers with slender, yellow petals appear in summer; constantly moist, well-drained soil; full sun to light shade.

BUTTERFLY WEED, MILKWEED
Asclepias **spp.**
24–48 inches tall
Zones 3–9
Several species and varieties with milky sap and butterfly-attracting flowers; spreading perennials with pink, orange, or yellow blooms in summer; milkweed is eaten by monarch butterfly caterpillars.

CARDINAL FLOWER
Lobelia cardinalis
36 inches tall
Zones 3–9
Glossy, green leaves; bright red spikes of flowers in summer also attract hummingbirds; different varieties have white to deep pink flowers; forms spreading clumps, but often lives for only a few years; grow in moist to sodden soil.

Enticing Birds to the Water Garden

Songbirds enliven the garden with music and flashes of color. Invite birds to your garden and you will never tire of their amusing antics as they search for food and mates and defend their nests. Insects are the preferred food of many bird species, such as swallows, flycatchers, chickadees, bluebirds, orioles, purple martins, and warblers, making them very desirable tenants in your yard. Give these birds the hunting habitats they prefer. Swallows swoop low over the surface of ponds to scoop mosquitoes and flies from the air. Kingfishers and other flycatchers, on the other hand, sit on a low branch or post to survey the area before diving on their prey. Warblers prefer brushy thickets near water in which to hide.

Nearly all birds enjoy bathing in water. Some splash in shallow puddles or in the water at the edge of a beach. Dripping water attracts others, and some fly through misting fountains. Build your pond or stream to include different kinds of bathing areas for birds to entice the greatest variety of species. Adding plants and shrubs nearby for food, nesting, and shelter makes your pond even more enticing. Berry-producing shrubs and trees are especially attractive. 🌸

BIRD-FRIENDLY POND

Create a diverse habitat that invites a variety of birds. Dripping water and shallow puddles provide bathing opportunities. Landscape with shrubs, trees, or other natural perches that provide food, shelter, and resting places. Add flowering plants to attract hummingbirds and add color to the garden. Hang birdhouses nearby. ❧

HAVE ON HAND:

- Preformed pond
- Spray paint
- Shovel
- Sand
- Carpenter's level
- Stone for edging
- Shallow basin with spout
- Drill and masonry bit

- Flexible black tubing
- Silicone caulk
- Submersible pump
- Water source

Plants

- 3 yellow and orange daylilies
- 3 garden phlox
- 1 black-eyed Susan
- 1 summersweet

Place preformed pond on ground. Mark outline of pond base on ground with spray paint. Set preformed pond aside.

Mark a new perimeter 18 inches beyond pond outline made in Step 1. Excavate entire area 4 inches deep; line area with 2 inches of sand.

Set preformed pond on sand; level. Lay courses of stone on sand around pond, using the top course to conceal lip of liner.

Place shallow basin on stones at one corner of pond. Direct spout so water will flow into pond. Drill hole for tubing in back of basin.

Place tubing in hole and seal around opening with silicone caulk. Attach tubing to pump, place pump in pond. Fill pond with water.

Plant the yellow and orange daylilies 24 inches apart along one side of pond.

Plant the garden phlox and black-eyed Susan across from the daylilies. Space them 24 to 30 inches apart to allow room for growth.

Plant the summersweet as a background shrub. Allow 4 feet on all sides. Water all plants well.

HERE'S HOW

PREVENTING PREDATORS

Herons, kingfishers, turtles, and raccoons pose the greatest predatory threat to your pond fish. Knowing their hunting habits helps you deter them. Kingfishers dive from a high perch, such as a utility wire or tree branch, into the water to capture their prey. Avoid placing your pond under a handy kingfisher perch, if possible. If necessary, cover the pond with a net.

The other predators wade into the water from dry land. Beaches and shallow planting shelves invite them to walk right in. Deep ponds with straight sides deter these animals. If raccoons are a nuisance, remove logs and stones that give them access to the water. You can also plant the pond perimeter densely with cattails and other marsh plants.

Alternatives

ATTRACTING HUMMINGBIRDS

Hummingbirds feed almost continually from dawn to dusk on flower nectar and small insects. They find red and other brightly colored, tube-shaped flowers attractive, but will feed from many other flowers, too. The gardens they like best offer shelter, water, and blooms throughout the season in which they visit. Their favorite flowers include gladiola, canna, agastache, bee balm, sages, lobelia, foxglove, zinnias, and trumpet and honeysuckle vines. Flowering trees and shrubs, such as horse chestnut and buckeye, black locust, tulip tree, flowering quince, fuchsia, lilac, and hibiscus, offer shelter as well as nectar-rich blooms.

Constantly on the go, hummingbirds even bathe on the wing. They enjoy flying through a fine misting spray from a fountain. Plant a shrub or small tree with narrow branches near the water to provide a perch on which the active birds can rest for a moment.

Males and females stake out territories and drive other hummingbirds away. To welcome a larger number of hummingbirds, divide your garden into "rooms" and separate them with screens, such as vine-covered trellises and tall shrubs. 🌸

BIRDBATHS

Even the very smallest water feature attracts birds, and you can ensure their visits by offering them water just the way they like it. By providing water year-round, especially when natural supplies are scarce, you will bring many species to your yard. In freezing winter climates, use a birdbath heater to thaw shallow, ice-covered containers. Add a low, trickling fountain or slowly dripping hose to entice them.

The best birdbaths offer a dry perch or edge on which to land and very shallow water that gradually deepens. Water depth that increases from ½ to 2 inches is ideal. It's also important to give birds a sense of security while they drink and bathe. Place the birdbath at least 3 feet off the ground if it's located near shrubs and other places where predators can hide.

Keep the birdbath and water clean to prevent the visiting birds from spreading diseases among themselves. It's a good idea to scrub and disinfect weekly, especially in warm weather. Be sure to rinse it thoroughly before returning it to the garden. Choose a birdbath that's easy to clean and offers secure footing so that birds don't slip. 🌸

Adding Goldfish to the Pond

Relaxing and fun to watch, goldfish glide hypnotically through the water and can be trained to come for food. Goldfish eat insects, keeping mosquito populations in check. They also scavenge the bottom of the pond looking for snails, worms, and bits of plants. Their waste adds valuable plant nutrients.

Goldfish need cool, clean water with plenty of oxygen to remain healthy. Deep ponds of at least 24 inches, in partial shade, maintain cooler, more stable water temperatures than shallow or aboveground pools, making them a better choice for fish. A pump attached to an aerating fountain also helps cool the water and adds much-needed oxygen. Unless your pond is large and the fish population very low, plan to add a filter. You can usually add about 2 inches of fish per square foot of water surface to a well-established pond, but remember that goldfish can grow rapidly to 12 inches in length.

Provide shelter from the sun and predators with overhanging rocks, logs, or floating plants. Goldfish can remain year round in ponds that do not freeze solid if you maintain a hole in the ice with a pond heater. Never keep goldfish in ponds where they could escape into the wild. ❧

INTRODUCING FISH

Comets, shubunkins, and other gold-fish with long bodies and single tails are hardiest and most suitable for pond living. When you choose goldfish, look for plump, active fish without clamped or ragged fins, skin lesions, or wounds. Avoid purchasing from an aquarium containing dead or unhealthy fish, even if some look okay. When adding new fish to an existing population, always quarantine the newcomers in separate quarters for at least a week. 🐟

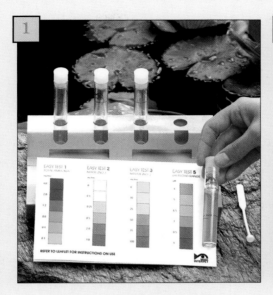

Test water chemistry for pH, ammonia, and nitrites to ensure a healthy fish environment. Replace some water to adjust, as necessary.

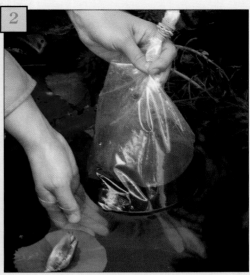

Float the plastic bag containing the fish in the pond for at least 1 hour to let water temperatures in the bag and in the pond equalize.

Open bag and let some pond water mix with bag water to let the fish gradually adjust to the new water chemistry. Allow at least 1 hour.

Release the fish into the pond. After 2 to 3 days, begin feeding only the amount that fish will eat completely in less than 5 minutes.

HAVE ON HAND:

▶ Water test kit

▶ Goldfish in a plastic bag filled with water

Wetland Gardens

Poor drainage usually signals soil compaction and problems for gardeners, but a naturally boggy site holds the promise of a wetland garden. The lists are long for plants that like excessive moisture, including many that prefer growing with their feet frequently flooded or continuously under water. The first project in this section shows you how to transform a damp or swampy swale from a liability into an asset in your landscape. You'll see, step by step, how to give a new look to a poorly drained site or waterlogged low spot. Besides improving its appearance, the new plants will also attract birds and butterflies.

In natural settings and in medium- to large-sized water gardens, plants that naturally grow in ponds, marshes, or at the water's edge help maintain an ecological balance, contribute color and texture, and blend with landscaping around the pond. You can enjoy the striking foliage and delicate blossoms of these handsome plants even if you don't have access to a piece of damp ground. Nearly all of them can grow in containerized minigardens on a deck or patio for close-up viewing.

The last project is a specialized one guaranteed to fascinate children, gardeners, and do-it-yourselfers. Here you'll encounter the intriguing world of carnivorous plants and learn how to build a perfect home for them. ❧

Creating a Natural Wetland Garden

Take advantage of the low spots, streams, and springs where pockets of moist soil remain damp, either seasonally or year round, and plant moisture-loving perennials, shrubs, and trees. Many birds, butterflies, and other small creatures depend on these natural wetland habitats for food and shelter.

After considering your sun and shade patterns, soil moisture, and desired maintenance level, decide on a theme for your wetland garden, such as floral display, wildlife attracting, or winter color and shapes. Some plants need shade, while others prefer sun. If the soil moisture varies through the year, look for plants that tolerate your soil conditions.

Trees, shrubs, and hardy perennials require less upkeep than annual flowers. Plan for low-, medium-, and tall-growing species as well as for plants that have flowers or other interesting features at different times of the year. Serviceberry, for example, has white, early spring blooms; red, bird-attracting berries; yellow autumn foliage; and smooth, gray bark. Other attractive shrubs for wet sites include alder, elderberry, red twig dogwood, viburnum, sweet bay magnolia, and winterberry. When choosing perennials, avoid plants that dominate or take over marshes in your area. 🌿

PLANTING A SWALE

To create an artificial wetland, install a flexible pool liner to keep the soil perpetually moist and add a perforated pipe for watering ease. Fill the liner with humus-rich soil to encourage lush plant growth. Choose plants for moist to saturated soil, as desired. Maintain soil moisture, especially in arid climates. Blend the wetland into the landscape by surrounding it with shrubs and other plants that grow naturally in your area. ❧

HAVE ON HAND:

- ▶ Spade
- ▶ Flexible pool liner
- ▶ Scissors
- ▶ Sharp knife
- ▶ 2-inch PVC pipe
- ▶ PVC elbow joints
- ▶ Drill and bit
- ▶ Tape measure
- ▶ Handsaw
- ▶ Garden hose connector
- ▶ Waterproof, nontoxic glue
- ▶ Pea stone or gravel
- ▶ Topsoil
- ▶ Moisture-loving plants

Dig a hole 2 to 3 feet deep in the desired shape and size of your wetland garden. Slope the sides slightly for greater stability.

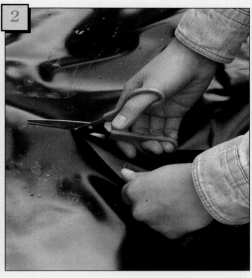

Line the excavation with flexible pool liner, trimmed so that it overlaps the sides by about 12 inches.

To aid surface drainage, use a knife to perforate the liner in several places, about 12 inches below the top.

Construct an irrigation system from 2-inch PVC pipe. Cut one section equal to length of garden. Perforate every few inches with drill and bit.

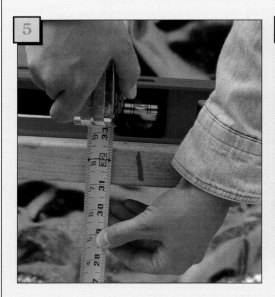

Cut another pipe equal to the garden depth. Cut the last piece to reach from the upright pipe to edge of the garden.

Connect pipes with elbows. Cap the end of the perforated piece and add a garden hose connector to the other open end. Glue together.

Spread 1 to 2 inches of small stone in the bottom of the garden. Install the perforated pipe and cover with another inch or two of small stone.

Fill garden with topsoil. Plant with moisture-loving calla lilies, primroses, spiderwort, water iris, and marsh marigold. Cover liner with stone or bark.

HERE'S HOW

PREVENTING MOSQUITOES

Mosquitoes lay their eggs in stagnant water, where they hatch into wriggling larvae. When mature, juvenile mosquitoes emerge from the water to look for warm-blooded prey. To keep mosquitoes from infesting your pond, add goldfish or mosquito fish, which eat the eggs and immature wrigglers.

To control mosquitoes in ponds too small to house fish, add a product called a mosquito dunk. The round disks contain a naturally occurring bacterium that kills mosquito larvae. It is not toxic to fish or any other animals.

Alternatives

PLANTS FOR SUNNY WETLANDS

Many of our most familiar wetland plants, especially those that grow in marshes and bogs, prefer full sun—at least 6 hours of sun during the growing season. Wetland plants usually need soil that remains moist year-round and will suffer if the soil becomes dry for part of the year. Add irrigation to your wetland garden, if necessary, during the dry months.

Choose species that are native to your area to provide needed bird and butterfly habitat, and make the garden look natural. State and local conservation organizations distribute lists of native plants and often sell plants inexpensively at fund-raisers. Use moisture-loving shrubs and trees such as cranberry bush, willow, winterberry, hackberry, or river birch to anchor and frame the garden.

Perennials offer a wide range of flower colors and leaf textures. Good choices include aster, goldenrod, bee balm, boltonia, bugbane, milkweed, marsh marigold, buttercup, rose mallow, spiderwort, cardinal flower, lady's mantle, and ferns. To keep creeping grasses from overgrowing your garden, surround it with a barrier, such as plastic lawn edging, and mulch with shredded bark or leaves.

PLANTS FOR SHADY WETLANDS

Shade occurs in different forms, from filtered shade under high-branched trees to dense shade on the north side of walls and buildings. Plants that grow in damp woods under the high canopy of trees usually prefer dappled shade for most of the day. Shrubs that naturally grow in the shade of larger trees include witch hazel, rhododendron, azalea, summersweet, red chokeberry, and spicebush.

If you want to add shade to a wet place in the yard, consider these trees: red and silver maples, larch, tupelo, bald cypress, sweet gum, and white and black spruces. White cedar makes a good screen or hedge shrub for damp soil, too. Create temporary shade with a lattice pergola until the trees become large enough to take over the job.

Many perennials thrive in moist shade, especially in otherwise hot summer climates. For outstanding foliage effects, try some of the many hosta varieties offered at garden centers. Flowering perennials for moist shade include astilbe, Dutchman's-breeches, lungwort, primrose, trillium, jack-in-the-pulpit, lily of the valley, sweet woodruff, umbrella plant, Virginia bluebells, Solomon's seal, ligularia, and goatsbeard.

Growing Marsh Plants in a Pot

Potted plants brighten patios and balconies with spots of colorful bloom, texture, and cool green leaves. Annual and perennial flowering plants fill traditional patio planters, but consider marsh and aquatic plants for your deck, too. In small yards and patios, a water garden can be as simple as a watertight pot planted with moisture-loving arrowhead, canna, blue flag, cattails, dwarf lotus, or rushes. Clustering pots can create the illusion of a larger water garden, even though the plants grow separately.

Clustered pots allow each plant to shine in its own environment and in concert with others. Use shallow containers for marsh and bog plants and urns up to 30 inches deep for water lilies. Plant some containers with tall marsh and low trailing plants, others with water lilies or lotus. Combine your small aquatic gardens with terrestrial container gardens and potted shrubs to create a complete aboveground landscape.

Add a bubbling fountain in a separate urn for soothing sound and dramatic effect. Mix different containers, such as ceramic pots, wooden barrels, and decorative urns, for an eclectic look or choose pots of similar style for unity. Be sure that containers do not leach metals, rust, or chemical residues into the water. ❦

POTTED MARGINAL PLANTS

Plant Japanese iris, sweet flag, arrowhead, and other marsh plants in a watertight container. Set a shallow liner on top of supporting concrete blocks. Pot up plants individually and set them in the water-filled liner. Choose a sturdy location for the container, which may weigh several hundred pounds when filled, and surround it with pots of flowering or foliage plants. 🌿

HAVE ON HAND:

- Large barrel
- Concrete blocks or bricks
- Two 10-inch-diameter plastic pots
- Heavy topsoil or aquatic plant potting mix
- Aquatic-plant fertilizer tablets
- Trowel

- ½-inch smooth gravel or pea stone
- Water source and hose

Plants
- 2 variegated sweet flag
- 2 arrowhead
- 1 iris laevigata
- 1 Japanese iris

Position a barrel in a sunny place on the ground or on a sturdy patio or deck.

Put concrete blocks or bricks in the bottom of barrel to evenly support two 10-inch pots.

Plant 2 variegated sweet flag and 2 arrowhead in heavy topsoil (no peat) in a 10-inch pot. Keep soil level 2 inches below rim of pot.

Plant the two kinds of iris in another 10-inch pot using the same soil mix. Keep soil level 2 inches below rim of pot.

Push 1 or 2 aquatic-plant fertilizer tablets into the soil of each potted plant. The tablets should be near the bottom of the containers.

Cover the soil with a layer of smooth, ½-inch stone to hold the soil in place. Keep stone away from new plant growth.

Arrange the plants on the bricks in the prepared barrel so that the lips of pots are about 4 inches below the lip of the barrel.

Fill barrel with water to within 2 inches of top. Plants should have 1 to 2 inches of water covering surface of soil.

HERE'S HOW

HARDY WATER LILIES

Most hardy water lilies grow from horizontal rhizomes. Although several types exist, you can plant them all the same way. If repotting or planting a new bare-root water lily, trim off most of the leaves and roots. Cut away any old or decayed rhizome, leaving a healthy piece up to 3 inches long.

Fill a 5-gallon pot three-quarters full of heavy topsoil, placing 1 or 2 fertilizer tablets in the bottom. Put the cut edge of the rhizome against the side of the pot with the growing tip angled up to where the soil surface will be. Fill with soil, keeping the tip just above the surface. Cover soil with ½-inch-diameter pea stone, avoiding the plant tip. Submerge in water up to a foot deep. Move the pot to deeper water when leaves begin to grow.

Alternatives

PAPYRUS

Ancient Egyptians used the stems of papyrus to make paper, but now this and others of its species are among the most popular ornamental water garden plants. Papyrus plants bear grasslike leaves, which resemble the spokes of an umbrella, at the top of stiff stems. Tufts of green or brown flowers form at the top of the stems in the summer. Papyrus plants grow year-round in moist to wet soil in tropical climates. In cold-winter climates, they will live indoors.

The smallest papyrus that's commonly grown in water gardens reaches only 12 to 18 inches tall. It spreads by bending its leafy tops into the water, where they take root and form new plants. The umbrella palm has several varieties that grow from 1 to 3 feet tall. 'Variegatus' has white-striped leaves and stems. Plant these papyrus species in pots and take them indoors before frost occurs.

For water gardens in Zones 9 or 10, where frost rarely or never occurs, consider Mexican papyrus or Egyptian paper reed. These species grow up to 15 feet tall and form large root clumps. Give them fertile soil at the edge of the pond in sun to part shade. ❧

A MINIATURE MARSH

Marsh plants are most at home in fairly shallow water or around the margins of a natural bog. But they also grow cheerfully in artificial ponds and container gardens as long as you provide them with continuously damp soil or up to 4 to 6 inches of water over submerged pots. To create a miniature marsh, choose plants with restrained growth habits that provide interest throughout the warm season. If you have enough space, begin with the pert spring blooms of marsh marigold and follow with golden club. Or opt instead for the sure-to-please summer blooms of a vibrant white tulip lotus, such as 'Shirokunshi', which reaches only 18 inches high. For a fanciful show from summer through fall, add the white blooms of star rush dancing above grasslike foliage.

To block sunlight and prevent algae from growing in a minigarden, be sure to include small floating plants that don't require potting. Nearly vertical rosettes of tropical water lettuce look velvety and invite touching. For a contrasting shape, add rounded floating foliage of frogbit or the bronze and green sculpted leaves of water clover. Foliage of these eventually covers the surface. ❧

Creating a Bog Garden

Bog plants grow in very acidic, moist to wet, infertile peaty soil. Many bog plants have developed unique ways to obtain the nutrients they need to grow. Carnivorous plants, for example, trap insects with specialized leaves. Bog plants' unique requirements and habits make them fascinating specimens for container gardens.

Shallow, waterproof containers, such as a window box, hypertufa trough, half-barrel, or ceramic pot, make ideal above-ground bog gardens. You can also make an in-ground bog with a pool liner or even a child's wading pool. Depending on your climate and the container and plants you choose, you can keep the plants in separate pots and sink them into the artificial bogs or plant them directly in the soil. Leave plants in separate pots if they must be moved for winter storage.

Put your bog garden in full sun in most climates, but offer midday shade if you garden where the sunlight is especially intense or the humidity level is low. To prevent the buildup of mineral salts in the soil, it's important to use water with a low mineral content, such as rain- or distilled water, especially if you live in a hard-water area.

CARNIVOROUS PLANTS

Bog plants grow in very moist to wet soil, so make this bog garden in a waterproof, patio-sized container. Drill holes through the container 2 to 3 inches below the soil surface to prevent flooding. Use a mix of sphagnum peat moss and washed sand to fill the container. Buy carnivorous and other bog plants from specialty nurseries. Do not purchase plants collected from the wild. ❧

HAVE ON HAND:

- Drill and ¼-inch bit
- Sphagnum peat moss, finely shredded
- Washed or play sand
- Trowel
- Plastic tub, for mixing
- Long-fiber sphagnum moss
- Rain- or distilled water, and gallon jugs
- Large plastic window box, 12 inches high and wide and 24 inches long

Plants
- 2 monkey cups
- 2 Venus fly-traps
- 3 round-leafed sundews

Drill several ¼-inch holes in the sides of the box about 3 to 4 inches from the top, preferably on the back or another hidden side.

For potting mix, thoroughly combine equal parts of sphagnum peat moss and clean sand in a plastic tub. Break up clumps and remove debris.

Stir in water until the mixture is nearly mud. Allow it to stand for a few hours if it resists wetting, and mix again.

Pack the wet potting mix into the window box to within an inch of the top.

Plant the monkey cups toward the back of container. Set the roots and crown into the soil at the same level at which they previously grew.

Plant the flytraps and sundews. Leave enough space between plants so that they can double in size without touching.

Soak long-fiber sphagnum moss until wet, and gently pack a ¹/₂-inch-deep layer around the plants, covering the surface of the soil.

Drench with distilled water (to prevent mineral buildup) until water runs out side holes. Top up as necessary. Trim damaged and decaying leaves.

HERE'S HOW
WATER PLANT PESTS

Many insects, including aphids and the larvae of many beetles and moths, feed upon water plants, disfiguring and weakening them. Look for chewed holes and skeletonized and disfigured leaves. Japanese beetles also attack waterside plants.

To control most insect pests, remove the affected leaves and keep the pond clear of decaying vegetation. Look under leaves for insects and their eggs and wipe off or spray with a strong jet of water. Avoid harmful insecticides, which may kill fish and other aquatic creatures.

Pond snails, which lay long, jellied egg masses on leaves and stems, and some turtles also eat plant leaves. Quarantine new plants to prevent accidental snail infestations and wipe off egg masses.

Alternatives

PLANTS FOR A BOG GARDEN

Marsh plants often grow wherever the soil is moist for at least part of the year, but bog plants require more specific growing conditions. Perpetually moist to wet, acidic soil characterizes the natural habitat of bog plants. Bog-dwelling plants also enjoy at least 5 to 6 hours a day of full sun. Growing bog plants in containers is the easiest way to provide the habitat that these fascinating plants need. Purchase only cultivated plants and never collect them from the wild, where many populations are dwindling.

Some bog plants capture and digest insects in or on their specialized leaves. Many carnivorous bog plants, such as butterworts, sundews, Venus flytraps, and pitcher plants, require a period of winter dormancy. Other bog plants, such as bearberry and cranberry, have glossy evergreen leaves and brightly colored berries that add distinctive beauty to an already unique garden.

Bog gardens don't require much fertilizer. If desired, you can mist the plants once every 5 to 8 weeks with an orchid or acidic plant fertilizer that is diluted to one-quarter its normal strength. Use only rain- or distilled water to water your bog plants, unless your tap water is chlorine and flouride free and naturally very low in minerals.

AUSTRALIAN SUNDEW
Drosera adelae
4–6 inches tall
Zones 10–11
Long, lance-shaped, reddish green leaves dotted with small sticky hairs form a loose rosette; white to reddish brown flowers in summer; sodden, acidic soil rich in peat or other organic matter; full sun; avoid fertilizers and pesticides.

BUTTERWORT
Pinguicula spp.
4–6 inches tall
Zones 3–11
Many temperate to tropical species; rosettes of smooth, sticky leaves form spreading colonies; white, yellow, or purple flowers in spring resemble violets; consistently moist soil and full sun; overwinter temperate species in a cold place when succulent autumn leaves form.

VENUS FLYTRAP
Dionaea muscipula
6–18 inches tall
Zones 8–10
Perennial of warm, sodden bogs with rosette of narrow, green leaves ending in claw-tipped pads. Inner surface of pads is reddish colored to attract insects. In early to midsummer slender, white flowers top slender stalks. Bright light and constant, even moisture.

ROUND-LEAFED SUNDEW
Drosera rotundifolia
1–4 inches tall
Zones 3–8
Spoon-shaped leaves form rosettes up to 5 inches in diameter; sticky hairs snare small insects; white to pink flowers; acidic, sodden soil and full sun; avoid fertilizers and pesticides; overwinter in a cold place when special autumn leaves form.

VEINED PITCHER PLANT
Sarracenia purpurea ssp. *venosa*
4–12 inches tall
Zones 6–11
Funnel-shaped, greenish purple leaves form rosette of rounded, water-filled pitchers accented with wavy-edged lips; pink to red umbrella-like flowers in spring; sodden, humus-rich soil; full sun; store in a cool place when leaves die back in autumn.

Glossary

ALGAE simple photosynthetic, primarily aquatic organisms including some seaweed, plankton, and diatoms. When environmental conditions are optimum, algae growth can rapidly accelerate, resulting in a population explosion called an algae bloom. Excessive algae growth in a water garden can be harmful to many organisms.

AQUATIC PLANT a general term used to denote any plant that thrives in a wet environment.

BENTOLITE a material made from bentonite and used as a water barrier in ponds too large to use a flexible liner.

BENTONITE a type of water-absorptive clay formed by the decomposition of volcanic ash.

BERM a rounded, raised bank of earth.

BOG a type of acidic, nutrient-deficient wetland composed of often-thick layers of partially decayed sphagnum moss.

BOG PLANT a plant adapted to living in a bog, although the term is often used to denote any plant able to thrive in a wet environment.

BUTYL RUBBER a type of synthetic rubber impervious to water; used to make flexible liners (water barriers) for water gardens and pools.

CARPENTER'S LEVEL a measuring device to determine true horizontal or vertical direction by centering a bubble in a vial partially filled with fluid.

CEMENT a mixture of limestone and clay that when mixed with water and aggregates, such as sand or stone, forms a bonding agent such as mortar or a building material such as concrete.

CONCRETE a substance made from cement, water, and any of a number of aggregates, such as sand, stone, or gravel, to form stonelike building materials such as concrete blocks.

ECOLOGY the relationship among organisms and their environment.

EPDM RUBBER (ETHYLENE-PROPYLENE) a type of synthetic rubber impervious to water; used to make flexible liners (water barriers) for water gardens and pools. EPDM rubber is resistant to ultraviolet rays and remains flexible in heat as well as in cold.

FAUX-STONE a concrete material resembling stone; used to make containers, birdbaths, and other garden accents.

FLEXIBLE LINER a pliant sheet, most often either 40 or 60 mil thick and usually made of polyvinyl chloride (PVC) or rubber; used as the water barrier along the bottom and sides of a water garden or pool.

FLOATING PLANT any plant, such as water lettuce and water hyacinth, that freely floats on the water surface.

FLOW REGULATOR a device, such as a clamp, that regulates the flow of water in a water garden or feature from a pump to an accessory such as a fountain or waterfall.

GROUND FAULT an imbalance in an electrical circuit where current follows an unintended path to ground.

GROUND FAULT CIRCUIT INTERRUPTER (GFCI) an electrical device often designed as part of an electrical outlet that detects ground faults. GFCIs shut off the current to the circuit as soon as a ground fault is detected, which helps prevent electrocutions.

HYPERTUFA a mixture of cement, water, sand, and peat moss used to create decorative containers for growing plants.

IN-GROUND POND a pond built by excavating a hole in the soil, and with the pond's upper rim flush or nearly flush with the surrounding ground.

JOINTING TOOL a mason's tool shaped like a mason's trowel but more narrow at the base and tapering to a point; used to remove excess mortar from between bricks, pavers, or stones.

KOI varieties of the common carp with brightly colored and patterned bodies often used in water gardens and ponds.

LANDSCAPE TIMBER a length of usually squared, most often quarter-sawn lumber used in the construction of landscape features such as steps and raised beds.

LOW-VOLTAGE LIGHTING decorative outdoor lighting powered by electricity of substantially lower voltage than normal household current.

MARGINAL PLANT any plant adapted to living in the shallow water at the edges of ponds and streams, such as cattails and arrowheads. Some marginal plants can also grow in wet soil above the waterline. Marginal plants are also called emergent plants.

MARSH PLANTS herbaceous plants, such as cattails, rushes, and sedges, that thrive in shallow water. Marsh plants differ from bog plants in that marsh plants grow in soil while bog plants grow in partially decomposed peat.

MORTAR a mixture of cement, water, and sand used as a bonding agent to secure building material such as stones, bricks, tiles, and pavers.

OXYGENATING PLANT any aquatic plant that helps aerate and purify the water of a pond or stream by adding oxygen to the water.

PH the measure of hydrogen ions in a solution that is used to express the solution's acidity or alkalinity on a logarithmic scale from 0 to 14 with 7.0 being neutral. Values below 7.0 are acid while those above 7.0 are alkaline. The preferred pH for most water gardens is between 6.8 and 7.4.

POLYVINYL CHLORIDE (PVC) a plastic resin impervious to water used in the manufacture of a number of products including water pipes and rigid pool liners.

PREFORMED LINER a rigid water garden or pool water barrier prefabricated of molded plastic, fiberglass, or other material and used in place of a flexible liner.

PUMP CAPACITY the volume of water moved through a water pump over a set period of time. Pumps used in water gardens have their capacity expressed in gallons per hour (GPH).

REBAR steel bars of varying diameters used to reinforce concrete.

SLOPE the amount of vertical drop between two fixed points.

SPHAGNUM MOSS a type of peat moss commonly found growing in bogs in the Northern Hemisphere and used as a soil amendment, an ingredient in many soilless mixes, or as a growing medium for bog plants.

SUBMERGED PLANT a plant growing entirely or nearly entirely beneath the surface of a pond or stream and rooted in the sediments of the bottom of the body of water.

SUBMERSIBLE PUMP a water pump designed to operate while completely immersed in water.

SWALE a low, usually wet area surrounded by higher, often well-drained land.

TRANSFORMER an electrical device that most often lowers the voltage of an electrical current without altering its frequency.

UNDERLAYMENT the material, often made of geo-textiles, that is installed beneath the flexible liner of a water garden to protect the liner from punctures.

WATER FILTER a device, either mechanical or biological, that purifies the water in a pool or water garden by removing particulates and toxic substances. Mechanical filters use fine grade materials, such as foam, to strain the water of unwanted materials. Biological filters use living organisms, such as bacteria, in combination with some inorganic aids, such as sand, to strain and detoxify the water.

WATER PLANT a general term used to describe a plant suitable for use in a water garden; includes plants classified as marginal, submerged, and floating.

Index

TIME® LIFE BOOKS

Time-Life Books is a division of Time Life Inc.
Time-Life is a trademark of Time Warner Inc. and affiliated companies.

TIME LIFE INC.
CHAIRMAN AND CHIEF EXECUTIVE OFFICER: Jim Nelson
PRESIDENT AND CHIEF OPERATING OFFICER: Steven Janas
SENIOR EXECUTIVE VICE PRESIDENT AND CHIEF OPERATIONS OFFICER:
    Mary Davis Holt
SENIOR VICE PRESIDENT AND CHIEF FINANCIAL OFFICER: Christopher Hearing

TIME-LIFE BOOKS
PRESIDENT: Larry Jellen
SENIOR VICE PRESIDENT, NEW MARKETS: Bridget Boel
VICE PRESIDENT, HOME AND HEARTH MARKETS: Nicholas M. DiMarco
VICE PRESIDENT, CONTENT DEVELOPMENT: Jennifer L. Pearce

TIME-LIFE TRADE PUBLISHING
VICE PRESIDENT AND PUBLISHER: Neil S. Levin
SENIOR SALES DIRECTOR: Richard J. Vreeland
DIRECTOR, MARKETING AND PUBLICITY: Inger Forland
DIRECTOR OF TRADE SALES: Dana Hobson
DIRECTOR OF CUSTOM PUBLISHING: John Lalor
DIRECTOR OF RIGHTS AND LICENSING: Olga Vezeris

WATER GARDENS
DIRECTOR OF NEW PRODUCT DEVELOPMENT: Carolyn M. Clark
NEW PRODUCT DEVELOPMENT MANAGER: Lori A. Woehrle
EXECUTIVE EDITOR: Linda Bellamy
DIRECTOR OF DESIGN: Kate L. McConnell
PROJECT EDITOR: Jennie Halfant
TECHNICAL SPECIALIST: Monika Lynde
PAGE MAKEUP SPECIALIST: Jennifer Gearhart
DIRECTOR OF PRODUCTION: Carolyn Bounds
QUALITY ASSURANCE: Jim King and Stacy L. Eddy

Printed in U.S.A.
10 9 8 7 6 5 4 3 2 1

Produced by Storey Communications, Inc.
Pownal, Vermont

President	Pamela B. Art
Director of Custom Publishing	Megan Kuntze
Editorial Director	Margaret J. Lydic
Art Director	Cindy McFarland
Project Manager	Gwen W. Steege
Book Editor	Vicki Webster
Horticultural Editor	Charles W.G. Smith
Photo Coordination	Giles Prett, Cici Mulder, Erik Callahan, Laurie Figary
Book Design	Jonathon Nix/Verso Design
Art Direction	Mark A. Tomasi
Photo Stylist	Sheri Lamers
Production and Layout	Jennifer A. Jepson Smith
Indexer	Nan Badgett/Word·a·bil·ity
Author	Rosemary McCreary
Primary Photography	Kevin Kennefick

Additional photography on pages, as follows: (Gay Bumgarner (40, 77 right); Crandall & Crandall (28, 35 left, 43 right, 90, 106); Alan & Linda Detrick (57 right, 69 left); (Ken Druse (74); Christine DuPuis (115 right top, 115 right bottom); (Derek Fell (Brickman Group Design) (6, 31 left, 31 right, 65 right, 82, 86, 101 right, 102, 105 left, 105 right, 109 right, 119 right, 124, 127 left, 127 right, 131 left); Roger Foley (16, 48, 50, 53 left, 54, 72, 78, 94, 110, 119 left); gardenIMAGES (85 left, 109 left); Marge Garfield (132, 135 right bottom, 135, right upper middle, 135 right top); H. Armstrong Roberts (101 left); Holt Studios International (62); (Lilypons Water Gardens (89 right upper middle, 93 right upper middle); Janet Loughrey (iv); Allan Mandell (39 right, 128, 131 right); J. Paul Moore (98); Jerry Pavia (32, 36, 39 right, 43 left, 66, 85 right, 120); Giles Prett/Storey Communications, Inc. (35 right, 44, 53 right, 65 left, 69 right, 112, 115 right upper middle, 115 right lower middle, 115 left); Positive Images (8, 12, 26, 77 left, 116, 122); Mark Turner (57 left).

Special thanks to the following for their help: Berkshire Botanic Gardens, Stockbridge, MA; Ward's Nursery and Garden Center, Great Barrington, MA.

School and library distribution by Time-Life Education,
P.O. Box 85026, Richmond, Virginia 23285-5026.

CIP data available upon request:
Librarian, Time-Life Books
2000 Duke Street
Alexandria, Virginia 22314

ISBN 0-7370-0627-7

Zone Map

ALASKA

HAWAII

Range of Average Annual Minimum
Temperatures for Each Zone

Zone	Temperature
Zone 1	Below -50° F
Zone 2	-50° to -40° F
Zone 3	-40° to -30° F
Zone 4	-30° to -20° F
Zone 5	-20° to -10° F
Zone 6	-10° to 0° F
Zone 7	10° to 20° F
Zone 8	20° to 30° F
Zone 9	30° to 40° F
Zone 10	40° to 50° F
Zone 11	50° to 60° F